A Better Life

A history of London's Italian immigrant families
in Clerkenwell's Little Italy
in the 19th and 20th Centuries

ISBN 978 0 904491 83 8

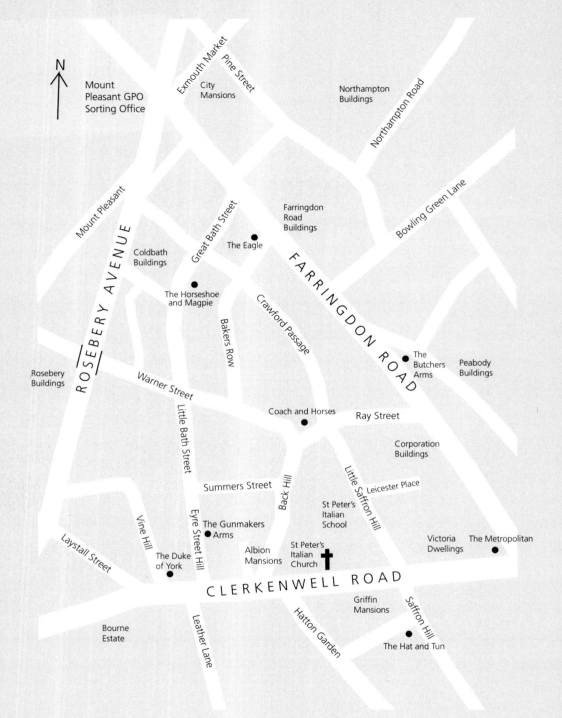

Map of the area known as 'Little Italy', c.1910,
based on a sketch map kindly researched by John Besagni.
Some of the streets, for example Great Bath Street, no longer exist.

A Better Life

A history of London's Italian
immigrant families
in Clerkenwell's Little Italy
in the 19th and 20th Centuries

Olive Besagni

Compiled by Olive Besagni, née Ferrari

Edited by F Peter Woodford

Designed by Ivor Kamlish

Preface

This collection of oral histories of the inhabitants of a district of London, since 1965 lying largely in the London Borough of Camden, differs from similar collections in that it records the histories of whole families, going back three or four generations or even farther into the 19th century, when a sizeable economic migration of Italians to Britain took place. Some of the histories have appeared before in the pages of Backhill, a monthly magazine produced for a community of Italians which became known throughout London as the Italian Quarter. (One of the principal thoroughfares in the Quarter was and is called Back Hill.)

The editor of Backhill from its inception in 1977 until 1998 was Francesco Giacon, who writes "Pino Maestri, a native of the Italian Quarter, made many contributions to Backhill under the heading of "The Hill" over the years. They provided a unique insight into the life and times of the families and residents of the quarter. His memorable walks around Little Italy describe the families who lived in the various streets and who enjoyed the good and the bad times of those now far-off days. Pino's great passion was football and he enjoyed recalling the games when his team, 'The Coach and Horses', enjoyed their successes in league and cup games."

When Pino died, Olive Besagni continued the work. She writes " I was never a resident of 'The Hill', as my parents had moved to Hampstead in the early 1920s. My grandfather, however, was known to many of the Italians, as he had been the headmaster of St Peter's Italian Night School. For more than 50 years he was known to all as Maestro Ferrari (p 153). When I married in 1948, my husband, Bruno Besagni, was still living in Victoria Dwellings, Clerkenwell Road. I decided that as I was a relative newcomer to the history of the Clerkenwell Italians, I would visit families and interview the oldest family member or descendants and get accounts of their immigration from the horse's mouth. The stories of the individual families illustrate the details and flavour of daily life 'down the hill'. The names resonate down the decades, with a few now remaining as a reminder of the once dominant Italian community, and others evoking memories of the days before the community dispersed."

The family histories are preceded by a historical overview of the migrations and the development of the Italian Quarter. One section describes the dominant influence of St Peter's Italian Church on the Clerkenwell Road and its associated schools. The source of each history, where it was not one elicited and recorded by Olive Besagni, is indicated at the head of each section.

Olive Besagni in 1985 at St Luke's Conference Centre
where her musical "Down the Hill" was being performed

Although what is defined in this book as Little Italy is partly in the modern borough of Islington and only partly in the London Borough of Camden, the Camden History Society has decided to publish the book without pedantically splitting the area according to current and past local authority boundaries. The Society is proud to bring this vibrant and affectionate account of a now less homogeneous, but still distinctly Italian, district to a wider audience.

F Peter Woodford
Editor, Camden History Society publications

Stores selling Italian food and wines were a well-known feature of Little Italy. Here is Basilia Mariani, often known as Mariana, presiding over such a shop in the 1930s. She and her husband Alfonso came from Minori (Southern Italy) and opened the shop in 1920. In the 1950s their son-in-law Pip Gazzano took over the shop with his wife Luisa (née Mariani) and it became known as Gazzano's; his son Joe Gazzano succeeded to the business and ran it with his sister Ruth; when he died in 2010 his son, another Joe Gazzano, took over and ran the shop with his wife Lucy. Gazzano's was still thriving at 167-169 Farringdon Road in 2011.

Contents

Acknowledgements

My heartfelt thanks to

Alison Sproston, for setting me on this path
and encouraging me along the way

Gerard Sproston for editing, proof-reading,
helping and supporting me

Simon Bratley for his work in collating
photographs

Bruna Redmond (née Maestri) my friend
and a source of great encouragement

My husband Bruno for his patience and
understanding

My daughters Anita & Nicolette, for
all their help, as well as my son Tony
and my grandsons Nick, Steven & Michael

Introduction by Olive Besagni

A friend of Italian extraction once told me an amusing story about his nephew, aged seven. Apparently in the course of a geography lesson, the class were asked if they knew where Italy was. The small boy excitedly put his hand up – "I know, Miss, my *Nonno* (Grandfather) comes from Italy, it's in Clerkenwell!" That story brings a smile to present and past Clerkenwellians. They remember the days when a small area of London's Clerkenwell was known to the English as Italian's Hill, or Little Italy. To the Italians it was known as "*Il Quartiere*" or "The Italian Quarter" or "The 'ill".

Over many decades articles, pamphlets and books have been written about Italian immigrants and their culture, but never a specific account of Clerkenwell's almost invisible immigrants who arrived in England in the early 19th century and settled there. Why so many Italians settled in this particular area of London is not clearly known. Early in the 19th century, when the terrain surrounding the small area that was Clerkenwell consisted of green fields with small farms, inns and manor houses dotted here and there, the earliest Italian immigrants trickled into the town. These early settlers were in the main young men from the mountainous regions of Northern Italy and Switzerland, usually the sons of families living on smallholdings with primitive living conditions, trying to escape the poverty trap of too many mouths to feed from too small a plot of land. As with all movements of peoples, they came looking for a better way of life, the chance to earn a living wage and eventually to return to their loved ones with riches to share. I wonder if they knew exactly where they were heading on their journey to a new land? The road they travelled was hard beyond belief. They had to walk most of the way, covering mountainous, rugged terrain, perhaps getting a lift on a hay wagon, stopping to sleep by the roadside, hungry at times and often weary at heart when their thoughts returned to their loved ones left behind.

Before 1844 there were no trains from Dover to London so our early immigrants, having already made their way across Italy through Switzerland and France, plus the channel crossing from Calais, had only vague ideas as to where they were heading. Having reached England they faced further endurance. They travelled on foot from Dover or Folkestone, perhaps getting a lift on a hay cart or, if they had any money at all, which was doubtful, a mail coach. If they were lucky and it was the fruit-picking time of the year, the fruit farms dotted around Kent may have provided them with food or a couple of days' employment. The Italians must have appeared strange to the English folk with their weird speech, dark hair, swarthy complexions and unusual mode of dress.

Alternatively they may have arrived on cargo boats via the Thames and disembarked at the London Docks, in which case, what sight of the promised land greeted them! One story often repeated was that as one man stepped off the gang plank at the London Docks, he kissed the ground and said *"Dio Grazie*, I've arrived in America!"*. I wonder how long it was before he was enlightened.

The dockland area would have been a scene of hectic activity with seamen of varying nationalities, rough dockers, wealthy merchants, warehouses, slums, unsavoury inns, drunken women, sailors sleeping it off in the gutters. The noise would have been horrific. However, there was always the possibility of a day's work in the docks, unloading the merchandise from the big ships onto the barges – hardly the stuff dreams were made of. There were of course signs of affluence: surrounding the docks were the homes of rich merchants, gentlemen's clubs, hotels and the trappings of the wealthy, but all this would mean to our immigrants was the possibility of a job, however menial. Tough as these men were, to have survived the journey to England alone or with other transient fellow countrymen whom they had met on their travels, the further journey across London must have been a nightmare, the stench of the horse dung, unfamiliar culinary aromas, slops and effluence running in the gutters, strangers going about their business, fighting, swearing amid the clatter of horses' hooves, the rattling and clanking of carriages as they tore around the narrow roads and alleyways. Did they realise then the great divide that separated the classes? You were either rich, getting by, or a member of the wretched poor, in this their new world.

We can picture Clerkenwell in this early part of the 19th century as an area of slums, a confusion of small lanes, hovels, and barefoot children, local citizens as hungry and destitute as the immigrants themselves, with no sign of the land of plenty that they had envisaged. Our immigrants would have experienced a London where thieving was rampant, where 'con' men, given the chance, would have robbed them of all they possessed. (In his novel *Oliver Twist*, Dickens gives us the picture that must have greeted their eyes, as Oliver is waylaid by the Artful Dodger and taken to Fagin's den, later fleeing from Bill Sykes along Saffron Hill, a street which later became central to the Italian Quarter.)

According to Terri Colpi's book *The Italian Factor*, few of the poorer immigrants who arrived in Clerkenwell in the early 1800s remained there. On the other hand, it is well documented that as early as the late 1700s some Italians with saleable skills – artists and gilders – lived in fine houses in Hatton Garden. Barometers dated between 1825 and 1830 are signed Comitti; Onerato Comitti (p 51) moved to Clerkenwell in 1845, possibly to join relatives residing there.

There were no Catholic churches in the area, as Catholicism was still under wraps (attitudes toward the faith were hostile and remained so until well into the 1870s); there were even guards at the doors while masses were celebrated. As the number of Italians in the area increased, Rome sent a young Italian priest to serve the Italian immigrants. Don Angelo Maria Baldacconi from Siena arrived in

London in 1824. His duties were not only to look after the Italians who attended mass at the Sardinian Chapel in Sardinia Street, Lincoln's Inn Fields, but also the English and Irish Catholics in the area.

The chapel was within walking distance from Clerkenwell. Irish immigrants, like the Italians, were attracted to an area where there were many cheap lodging houses, rather close to the West End. Baldacconi had his work cut out; there was desperate poverty in the area, and hunger and poverty begot crime, which was rife. There were no English state schools at the time. A small school attached to the Chapel was subsidized by the Piedmontese government. As the intake of Italian immigrants increased, illiteracy along with the language barrier created many problems. There were two prisons in the locality; the Middlesex House of Detention and Coldbath Fields Prison were terrible places where a miscreant, particularly a foreigner, would be confined for any number of reasons – for instance the theft of a loaf of bread. Many English or foreign street urchins over the age of 7 were sentenced to hard labour for minor offences. Without question, Baldacconi had a very heavy work load. He did his best, but it must have been distressing and very hard to maintain his faith while witnessing the harsh treatment of human beings: prisoners were either hanged or put on a convict ship and deported to Australia for really trivial offences.

In 1844 the first railway from London reached Dover and linked with the cross-channel steamers, giving later immigrants – if they had the money – the chance of a less arduous journey from the coast to their destination in London. However, as a great many were penniless they are known to have walked. It was known that some of the earlier immigrants had taken over small houses in Clerkenwell (close to Hatton Garden) where they would let out rooms to help pay the rent.

Here the men tried to find work, and those who succeeded would put aside enough to enable them to go back to their native village to reclaim their girlfriends or wives who, with their children, had sometimes waited years for the return of their menfolk – and with no way of knowing whether that would ever happen. Some Italians, on the other hand, married Irish girls who shared their faith.

By the 1850s there were about 2000 Italians in the area – mostly poor, unskilled peasants from the mountainous regions of Northern Italy – Piacenza, Parma, Borgo val di Taro, Morfasso and Bardi – and some from Italian-speaking Ticino in Switzerland. The majority were genuinely seeking honest work, God-fearing and needy, but among them were chancers and the odd bad character. Immigrants from other parts of Italy joined the exodus. Among them were *arrotini* (knife-grinders) from villages in the Trentino Region – semi-skilled labourers – many of whom walked the entire journey pushing the wheelbarrows that carried their grindstones and other knife-grinding equipment. From 1850 the Southern Italians from the *comuni* of Picinisco and Casalattica had joined the trail to the new country.

In 1861 the Italian Benevolent Mission was set up, with responsibility for repatriating distressed and destitute Italians who were unable to cope with the hard life of the immigrant. One of its main concerns, however, was with the young children who were being exploited by men who made them work for minimal wages, which they would then take back in rent for abysmal board and lodgings in overcrowded, dirty tenements owned or rented by the employer. The Mission's work in this field was instrumental, in collaboration with the British government, in bringing about the prohibition of begging in the streets by boys under the age of 14 and girls under the age of 16.

With the Italian presence in the area increasing rapidly, Baldacconi founded a free school in Leicester Place, Saffron Hill. Not surprisingly the overworked priest became ill and had to return to Rome, where he retired in 1843. His successor was Father Raffaele Melia, and Mass continued to be celebrated in the Sardinia Street Chapel. The job of looking after the two communities was immense. The Italians alone needed maximum attention as many were destitute, homesick and in frail health; repatriation was the only answer for some. The overworked priest was soon joined by a young priest, Giuseppe Faà di Bruno. These two good souls did their best to minister to the two communities, but over a long period and after much communication with Rome and with the backing of Vincent Pallotti – a young priest, later made a Saint – it became clear that the Italian community needed a church of its own. There followed years of fund-raising, negotiation, debates and disappointments and the death of Vincent Pallotti in 1850 caused further delays.

Detail of wall painting in the Chapel of St Vincent Pallotti in St Peter's Italian Church, showing the saint with Fathers Raffaele Melia and Giuseppe Faà di Bruno

St Peter's Italian Church

Now came the task of finding and purchasing an appropriate site. Further setbacks followed and it wasn't until the decision was made to build in Clerkenwell Road that plots of land became available and the site was finally purchased in 1852. The foundations of St Peter's were finally laid, though further funding was still required. Father Melia was recalled to Rome in 1856 where he was elected Rector General of the Catholic Apostolate, leaving Father Faà di Bruno to continue the work. After many setbacks, a church was built with a narrow frontage in Clerkenwell Road to designs by Irish architect Sir John Miller-Bryson that were based on the basilica of San Crisogono in Trastevere in Rome. It was consecrated on 16 April 1863. In the early days it was called 'The Church of all Nations', as it had been decreed that the church should be at the disposal of Catholics from every nation. The resident priests were always drawn from the Association of Pallottine Fathers. In the years that followed, other Catholic churches were built in the area, so this church became known as 'St Peter's Italian Church'.

At Christmas and Easter, the church would be packed to the doors, primarily with Italian and Irish families. A general cosmopolitan atmosphere prevailed. On these occasions the Church resounded to the sound of the 50-strong choir as they sang the Latin Mass and motets by Mozart and other great composers. There would be processions around the church headed by the priests wearing their vestments, followed by the altar boys swinging the thurible, spreading the sweet savour of incense. Little girls wore white dresses and scattered rose petals. In later years, numbers of Italians who had left the area would return

Interior of St Peter's Italian Church

to worship in the church on these Holy Days, when they would be reunited with relatives and friends.

Many young couples met at the Church dances where they went with the approval of their parents. In the building next to the Church, which is now the social club called *Casa Italiana S. Vincenzo Pallotti*, many social activities still take place, such as schools of card playing, dancing, snooker and social evenings.

Preparations for the Christmas Bazaar are carried on there all year round, some ladies knitting and crocheting while others prepare gifts for the tombola.

The façade of the church overlooking Clerkenwell Road is decorated with statues of Christ, St Bede and Saint George, and with two colourful mosaics of biblical scenes. In the porch is a plaque recalling the sinking of the *Arandora Star* by a German U-boat in 1940, with the loss of over 400 Italian internees, and the memorial is flanked by the names of those from the district who died in the First and Second World Wars, when Italy was fighting on the side of the British and the Germans respectively. The bell tower houses a huge single bell, the "steel monster", whose mournful *Boing, Boing, Boing* can be heard throughout Little Italy.

The community comes together

The Clerkenwell Italians were settling down into a close community, the unskilled men were finding work. London was growing and there was plenty of building going on. The asphalt, terrazzo, mosaic and ceramic trades, as well as restoration work, were popular with the Italians and a number of men worked on many of London's historical buildings. In 1870 there was an influx of semi-skilled workers, men from the Emilia Romagna regions, from Carrara, famous for its marble mountains, men already skilled in their craft. They included gilders, glass-blowers and men from Piacenza who were knowledgeable in the craft of mould making for the manufacture of plaster statuettes.

Ice cream cart in London park, c.1910. The saleswoman's costume is from the province of Frosinone

1878 saw the opening of St Peter's School in Little Saffron Hill (this Italian school had actually been founded earlier, in Hatton Garden). Most of the children attending the day school were Italian, but there were a few Irish, English and German children. There were also evening classes for illiterate adults, which would have offered many of them their first opportunity of an education.

The early entrepreneurs were plying their trades in the streets, ice cream makers in the summer, hot chestnut vendors in the winter, barrel-organs, buskers, sellers of statuettes on trays. The more enterprising would rent a small house and fill it with lodgers, each room sleeping a number of men – new arrivals, usually single men. More successful types started making seasonal visits to the home country for the harvesting, returning to England in the summer where, in the cooler climate, the harvest would be later. Even the poorest accommodation in London was preferable to the harsh cold of winters in the mountains. Still they came, families, brothers and sisters, other relations would soon follow, leaving behind relatives who would work their small plots of land.

Selling hot chestnuts (Graphic newspaper, 17 February 1923)

In 1884 an Italian business man living in London, Giovanni Ortelli, was visiting one of his Italian employees who was being treated in an English hospital. Although the patient was receiving every care and attention, he was clearly very unhappy; he couldn't make himself understood and no one could speak or understand his language. Ortelli decided that Italians should have a hospital of their own where doctors and nurses would be able to speak to the sufferers in their own language. He converted a house he owned at 41 Queen Square into a hospital, spending thousands of pounds on its equipment and staffing. It later expanded into the next-door house No.40 as well, and then round the corner into Boswell Street. The Italian Hospital continued to receive patients until 1989 and after it closed as it became the Italian wing of Great Ormond Street Hospital. Ortelli was rewarded with the title of *Commendatore* by the Italian Government. Many inhabitants of Little Italy had cause to be grateful for the existence of this hospital within walking distance of Clerkenwell. One of them even became one of its doctors (p 50).

Into the 20th century

There was now some order in the lives of the immigrant Italians. They had a church, a school, an active benevolent society and their own hospital: they were no longer invisible. Clerkenwell had become home. The awful travelling conditions between Britain and Italy had greatly improved, though channel crossings could still be quite unpleasant! Word had travelled across the valleys and the mountain ranges 'England was a good place to go'.

A set pattern emerged at this time. Those families already ensconced in their own small businesses were sending for relatives outside their immediate family to come and work for them. They trusted only immigrants from their own villages or region of origin and were unwilling to employ strangers. There was a great deal of movement from Tuscany, and the Tuscans began setting up in little shop fronts,

Eyre Street Hill, c.1919. Halfway up, women sitting outside the Gunmakers' Arms, aka Dondi's. Bottom right, Mrs Avella and daughter (p 125)

or houses, to manufacture plaster statues. There was an abundance of small family cafés, and the Italians appeared to be making the catering trade their own. At this time it was mainly the northern Italians, but it wasn't long before the Italians from the south jumped on the bandwagon. Life for the immigrants was beginning to take an upturn.

The first World War

The start of World War I in 1914 changed all that. The Italians fought side by side with Britain, some enlisting with the British Army while others returned to Italy to join the Italian Army. Those with language skills were employed by the British Government as interpreters. Some wives returned with their children to their villages in order to be near their menfolk. When the armistice was signed the men and their families returned to pick up their life, or what remained of it, in the Italian Quarter, and in some cases to make a completely new start.

The triangle between Clerkenwell Road, Rosebery Avenue and Farringdon

16

Road, with one or two streets and alleyways branching off it, had become known as the Italian Quarter. There is no doubt that it was a rough and frightening patch of London to the outsider. Some volatile young Italian men carried knives, ostensibly for their own protection, and there were sometimes violent fights amongst themselves. There was a period in the early days when the Italians living in the quarter felt threatened, and indeed they were. Areas surrounding the quarter, in the East End and even across the river in South London, had many street gangs who were aware of the vulnerability of these foreigners in Clerkenwell. They would converge on the Italian Quarter, beat and bully the men and boys, insult and take

Looking down Great Bath Street towards Eyre Street Hill

liberties with the young woman and girls; the residents were just as frightened of the police as they were of the gangs, and so had no one but their priests to turn to. This particular problem was solved by the merging of two families, the Cortesi brothers and the Sabini brothers, which started because a member of one of those outside gangs insulted a young woman working in a bar in one of the local pubs. Darby Sabini, who had a ferocious right hand, gave the man a good pasting. The young Italian men now had a leader, so that when the gang whose member Darby had beaten up returned for reprisals, the local youths, led by Darby and the Cortesis gave them what for. This ended the regular brutality that the Italians had previously suffered, as they felt they had some protection from the marauding gangs. Later on the Cortesis and the Sabinis quarrelled over pitches at horse races, and the resulting feud lasted for many years, during which these men were referred to as 'the Racing Fraternity'.

    Although I never myself lived in the Quarter, I was the granddaughter of Giovanni Ferrari (p 153), a master at the St Peter's Italian schools from 1880 to 1933 and eventually their director. His son Giuseppe (Joe) Ferrari, my father, moved out of the Quarter in the 1920s, I was born in Gospel Oak and moved to Constantine Road, Hampstead, when I was 11. Later I married a denizen of the Quarter, Bruno Besagni. The story of his remarkable mother Anita is told on pp 114-124. I began to be interested in the story of the Italians that I met through working in a statuette factory near the Quarter beginning in 1940, and from the time of my marriage in 1948 onwards, and asked them to recall the old days 'down the Hill'. Without exception they told me that whereas it was no easy life there, what they lacked in worldly goods was made up for by the love of family and friends. Neighbours' doors were always open, and no matter how large the family, another chair at the table would always be found for visitors and friends.

Most of those I interviewed readily conceded that up until the 1930s the Italian Quarter was little more than a slum. If you had two rooms you were well off. The Quarter consisted of some very large overcrowded blocks of flats such as Victoria Dwellings, a huge block on the corner of Clerkenwell Road and Farringdon Road, and the rather grandiosely named Cavendish Mansions further along Clerkenwell Road in a triangle between the back of Rosebery Avenue and the narrow passageway of Laystall Street. These flats were actually an improvement on the homes in the heart of the Quarter, comprising Saffron Hill, Back Hill, Eyre Street Hill, Ray Street, Warner Street and Summer (later Summers) Street, which contained smaller blocks of flats, small houses and old shops.

Some of the families actually lived in what had been a shop, while others lived above a shop selling goods that contributed to the Italian way of life: macaroni, coffee beans, tubs of olives, fish, many and various Italian cheeses, meats, salami, prosciutto, rough Chianti-style wine, and bread. Some of the provisions were made on the premises, with chickens and the occasional goat in the yard behind. These were the first of the Italian delicatessens, so popular today, and without exception were run by the immediate family. Alternatively they would set up a stove, a couple of tables and chairs and serve cups of tea or coffee, and plates of spaghetti. These little cafés would become meeting places where the customers, mostly men, would sit over a cup of tea, coffee or a glass of home-made wine and bread, playing cards, singing or simply whiling away the time. There were several clubs: the Fratellanza on the corner of Warner Street and Bath Street, and the Mazzini-Garibaldi Club at No.10 Laystall Street. Here in 1864 Giuseppe Mazzini welcomed Giuseppe Garibaldi to London. There were also the Lombardi Club in Summers Street and the Colonial Club, used by Italian workers, ice men, asphalt layers, and terrazzo workers. There was also the Italian Club run by Fuoco at No.20 Mount Pleasant, popular because of the *bocce* (bowling) lanes at the back of the premises.

The Procession

Second-generation Italians whose childhood was spent in the Quarter recall the happiest of times when life was fun. For the vast majority, life revolved around St Peter's School associated with St Peter's Italian Church.

The most exciting event of the year was the annual procession of Our Lady of Mount Carmel, always celebrated on the Sunday nearest to the 16th of July. The day has been celebrated by the community every year since 1896, interrupted only during WW II.

Children played an important role in the procession, the girls wearing white dresses with veils, the boys in white suits and carrying a lily, and the older lads in groups representing the Apostles, Roman soldiers or Papal guards, or wearing national costume. Men carried the heavy statue of Our Lady of Mount Carmel on a platform decked with flowers.

Houses and shops in the streets would have their own little altars outside and decorations, flowers mostly, or pictures of their favourite saint or a Madonna. There were flowers in abundance, carried in baskets and draped round the banners; rose petals were strewn in front of the statues by flower girls and hymns were sung with reverence and gusto. Everyone had their part to play; the *Mammas* having prepared food at home on tables laden with Italian delicacies also walking in the procession, usually wearing black.

In later years, an important part of the celebrations would be the arrival of the bands. One group in particular, remembered with affection, was the North Hyde Pipers who arrived on the Friday evening when the festivities would begin. Each evening they played in the streets at the heart of the Hill. When the band took a break there would always be an accordionist or two to keep things going, everyone would come outdoors and there would be dancing and singing until the early hours. The procession was a way of showing their pride in their Catholicism and their Italian identity. The local police stopped traffic for the time the procession took to move on a circular route from the church entrance in Clerkenwell Road into Eyre

Staff at the Italian School, 1923. Back row: Sig.na Zaccharini, Sig. Giovanni Ferrari (on staff 43 years (see also p 153) and awarded a silver medal by the Italian Government), Cav. Father Anthony (Vice-Director for the past 25 years), John Taylor (headmaster of day school for 35 years), Cav. Raffaele Terroni (hon. sec. of the school and also of the Benevolent Society, see also p 104). Seated: Sig.na M Chiapponcelli, Dorothy Nathan (Lady Inspector), Cav. Uff. R Allatini (Chairman) and Sig.na Balestreri (headmistress)

Street Hill, Great Bath Street, Farringdon Road, via a small turning across Hatton Garden leading into Leather Lane, back to Clerkenwell Road and into the Church. As the procession ended, the priest would come out onto the church steps and bless the huge crowd that had gathered there. As the blessing took place, the crowd would genuflect. Later in the day it would be open house in all the homes, relatives and friends would call and the food and wine would flow.

In the words of a reporter in *The Graphic* newspaper, in an article in 1923 headed "The Italian Colony in London and its many activities":

Long view of the annual Procession, the statue of Santa Lucia being carried by men of the Terroni family, with the man who commissioned the statue, Giuseppe di Falco, walking alongside

Go through Hatton Garden, where the diamond merchants are and cross over to the northern side of Clerkenwell Road and you'll find yourself in 'Little Italy'. In half a dozen typical streets, the houses and shops are all occupied by Italians. It looks a poor neighbourhood, but I got a suspicion that the neighbourhood is not as poor as it looks. The laughing and even boisterous children romping in the roadway had dirty faces and mostly wore ragged clothes, but their health and vitality were unmistakeable. In their games Italian boys and girls give vent to tremendous lung power. I am assured, moreover, that the rate of infant mortality in the colony is remarkably low – a tribute to the care and devotion of Italian mothers to their children. To see a characteristic Italian scene one should go to 'Little Italy' on the Sunday following July 16. This is the feast of Our Lady of Mount Carmel, to whom all Italians render devotions.

A Better Life

The early 1930s saw a change in the living conditions of the Italian immigrants. Life "down the Hill" had improved in many ways, even though to an outsider the area still looked like a slum. But with the passing years, in common with the most other Londoners, they struggled to be cleaner. Italian *Mammas* were proud and industrious and a vast amount of elbow grease was applied daily, particularly by the older daughters. Even the humblest little homes had the whitest of doorsteps, and clean, shiny windows. Inside the houses floorboards and stairs were scrubbed so clean that they were almost white. The children were well shod and, although their clothes were shabby, mostly *'and me dahns*, they were clean. The big families with their many children had turned a corner; the teenagers of the day, who had known abject poverty for most of their young lives, were working; the boys often as commis waiters, and the girls as waitresses in cafés. Although they were poorly paid and relied mainly on tips, their mothers encouraged them to take jobs in the catering trades: "People will always eat, so you will never go hungry".

The atmosphere in the quarter remained Italian. The sights and sounds and the smell of Italian cooking, tomato sauces, and broth, the pungent smell of garlic and tasty salami wafted in the air. Everywhere could be heard the sound of vociferous women, children at play, the noisy bantering of the *baloche* (idle terenagers), as they played dice on the corner of Eyre Street Hill and Warner Street; the strident singing of the *Mammas* giving vent to the folk songs and barrel-organ music constantly coming from Chiappa's, the organ maker; the noisy shouts of the men playing *Murra*, a game similar to the English game of sticks and stones and, above it all, the sonorous tolling of St Peter's Italian Church bell.

Italian men would seek work in the finest hotels and restaurants, places like the Strand, the Dorchester, the Savoy, and in ritzy nightclubs such as the Café de Paris and the Embassy. The most popular place to begin life as a commis waiter was the Ivy, a restaurant in London's West End where for decades the glitterati of the era have been seen.

Most of the Italians proved to be hardworking and reliable, and many quickly rose up the ladder of success. When dressed in the garb of their respective professions they could be very handsome and elegant, with a great deal of charm, and were soon promoted to the status of Head Waiter, Head Wine Waiter, First, Second or Third Chef, Manager and other lucrative positions. These jobs often afforded the chance to meet Royalty, VIPs, famous film stars and the darlings of London's theatre land, with many of whom they were on first-name terms. However, most of these jobs involved long and unsocial hours.

The young women also enjoyed jobs as waitresses in high-class restaurants, wearing a black uniform with a white pinafore and head band worn low on the forehead. These young women would walk home to Clerkenwell from the West End, usually in pairs, in the early hours of the morning. They were protected by the young men working in the same business also making their way home to the

Quarter. There would be plenty of joshing and teasing, but the girls knew that they were in no danger as the fellows knew their families, and respected them. Many of these youngsters would pair up and eventually marry.

The more artistically inclined lads would go into the statuette industry. There were several statuette factories in the area. Pagliai in Great Sutton Street was the largest and best of its kind. Hours would be from 8 am to 6 pm and after 6 pm you would see young lads from the age of 14 and upwards walking home from work along Clerkenwell Road. If they were casters or finishers they would be covered in white plaster, and even if they changed their clothes, the plaster would still be in their hair and eyebrows. The sprayers smelled of paint and would often have daubs of paint on their clothes. Some of the Hill youngsters quickly caught on to the trade and within a few years were opening up their own small factories in Clerkenwell. They were generally happy and earning well.

For the older Italians, life down the Hill meant they continued to live alongside their own kind. Some of the earliest Italian immigrants were happily married to Irish girls. In later years, when the male immigrants were earning enough to send back to Italy for their wives, girlfriends and other relatives, mixed marriages became fewer.

The quarter became steeped in Italian culture. The Italians' love of music was deep in their soul. In the early years mountain songs predominated for the Northerners, typically the music of the Alpine troops or of their home districts and villages. For most Italians harmony is second nature and in the mountains and valleys music would often be their only form of relaxation. Whenever Italian immigrants gathered, at weddings, banquets, in pubs or in clubs, they would sing their mountain songs with fervour, for instance *Mazzolin di Fiori* (Little bunch of mountain flowers) or *La Montanara* (The girl from the mountains). If you attended a wedding reception in the home of the bride, you would inevitably hear the sound of music, and if you followed it you would find some twenty men singing in a back kitchen or wherever they could sing without disturbing the other guests. Usually it was not long before the other guests would follow the sound and join in the singing – women and children alike, for they all enjoyed a good sing-song.

For the Southerners songs of love, the sea, the sun and the saints, for instance *Mamma* (Mother), *Santa Lucia* and *O, Sole Mio* (O, my Sun) were popular with young and old alike. Songs from the opera, the universal love of the Italian, reached British shores in the first place on the penny whistle, the least cumbersome form of instrument, later on the mouth organ, and, as the years went on, the diatonic accordion, which had buttons instead of keys. Then came the barrel-organ, loved by many and hated by others, carted around the streets, sometimes accompanied by a monkey. The arrival of the wind-up gramophone in the late 1920s brought the wonderful arias of Verdi, sung by Enrico Caruso, the most popular Neapolitan tenor, into their homes and their hearts. He fought a debilitating illness in his last years, dying at the height of his fame, aged 40.

Beniamino Gigli, the second of the great tenors, did not fill his place, nobody could, but, thanks to the constant improvements in sound recording, he became as popular. Great was the rejoicing when he sang at the Royal Albert Hall, and once he even appeared at St Peter's Italian Church, where he joined with the choir as they sang the Latin mass (p 72). Imagine the joy of the choir – they had sung with the master! There was not an empty place in the church, nor a dry eye in the house, on that wonderful day.

At the end of the era Bing Crosby and Rudi Vallee were the teenagers' idols. The Hill was alive with the whistling of *Peanuts*, *Pennies from Heaven* and

The Mexano Accordion Band

passionate tangos – *Jealousy*, for instance. The younger set also loved Italian popular music: Tino Rossi, etc: They had their own Mexano Band, containing ten accordionists! The band was run by Luigi Finella.

Most Italians born in the Quarter attended St Peter's School and the Italian Church. They sang in the choir or served at the altar. It was not uncommon for Italian women to go to mass daily unless they were working. *Mammas* in their homes would answer the solemn tolling of the church bell with: "I'm comin', I'm comin' (*vengo, vengo!*)" They spoke to their children in Italian, and their children would answer in cockney English, common to the neighbourhood, but with the giveaway rolling 'r', and "dahn" in stead of "down." For instance "down the road", became "dahn de rrroad." Some of the women never left the Quarter and as a result never spoke a word of English. Those who were employed in the more select jobs had a better chance of improving their speech but there was always a hint of an accent.

Family life flourished. Everyone, whatever their age, would be expected to be home for Sunday dinner, which began between 3 and 4 pm. The table would be laid with snow-white linen table-cloths, white table napkins and sparkling glasses; the wine, usually homemade, would look good against the white tablecloths. The first course would always be chicken broth with *vermicelli* or other small pieces of pasta, or another kind of soup. Finally, Papa would arrive back from his Sunday session in Lou Resteghini's pub, the Coach & Horses on the corner of Warner Street and Ray Street, or from his game of bowls in the yard behind Dondi's Pub. Papa was the only family member who was allowed to be late, usually arriving a little flushed. He would sit at the head of the table, ready to carve, and Mamma and the daughters would then serve up. The main course was chicken, roasted or boiled, with roast potatoes and greens. The dessert consisted of a large bowl of fruit in the centre of the table, followed by Italian cheeses.

At St Peter's Italian School religion played a major part in the curriculum, but sport was also on the agenda, at least for the boys. Headmaster Mr Taylor had a great love of football. Under his guidance the sporting side of the school thrived. Mr Taylor was succeeded in 1936 by Mr McGee and the school became famous for its athletic abilities while still putting on a good show on the football field. However, competitive sport took second place to lessons. The girls were academically ahead of the boys, not having the sports to distract them, except perhaps a gentle game of netball now and again. At quite an early age they attended dances in the school hall, closely watched by Sister Angela, who made sure that they kept a respectable distance – the length of a ruler – from the boys.

Family was important and the *Papas* strove to keep their boys out of trouble, as there was always an element of thuggery and gambling simmering just beneath the surface. Not only Italian girls were attracted to Italian boys, with their good looks, dark eyes and black hair; they were also excellent dancers. The boys would go quite far afield for their dancing, to Covent Garden, the Paramount in Tottenham Court Road or Beale's in Holloway Road.

The girls were allowed much less licence. A very close watch was kept on them to maintain their respectability (i.e. virginity). If a young girl became pregnant, whether or not with her consent (lodgers in the house would sometimes take advantage of an innocent daughter of the household) the family shame would be such that they would disown the daughter or send her back to Italy. The only way out was a shotgun wedding. As a result, many girls entered into unhappy marriages, but generally they would endure it. Once married, the family would accept them again.

St Peter's Italian Church was always kept busy with marriages, funerals, baptisms and Saints' Days. When an Italian boy or girl presented their parents with an English prospective partner, there would be no joy, but, after many arguments, the newcomer would usually be accepted. If they were not Catholics they would be expected to convert. If on the other hand the couples were from the same *paese*, the excitement would be great and the preparations and planning for the big day monumental. Most young couples lived with parents so, when the babies arrived, there would usually be a *Nonna* (grandmother) in residence to rock the babies to sleep with Italian lullabies: '*Nina nana*'. She was also the fount of all knowledge concerning childhood illnesses.

In the 1920s infant deaths were common and many families would lose a toddler to one of the common diseases such as diphtheria, scarlet fever or whooping cough, which were all rampant, however much the poor mothers fought against the dirt and unhygienic conditions. Many sad little funerals took place in

Notice that there is to be an Italian clinic at Pine Street

the church; the mothers were often too much in despair to attend their little one's funeral. The children developed bone diseases – rickets and osteomyelitis – which could mean a long stay in St Mary's Children's Hospital in Carshalton. To get there from Clerkenwell meant first a train then a bus ride, and after that a very long walk to the hospital. Only one parent would be able to make the visit, the other had to stay home to look after the siblings.

One of the worst things for the Italian Mammas was that the Italian Hospital in Holborn was not a suitable place to discuss general child welfare, and

Italian doctor and nurse at Pine Street Clinic

although they could use the Pine Street Welfare children's clinic, the staff there could not speak Italian. They did their best, but communication was poor – so imagine the rejoicing the day a notice went up outside the Clinic announcing in English and Italian that in future an Italian Clinic would be held there on Mondays from 10.30 am until noon. Young mothers were always unsure how best to treat their baby: were they under-feeding, over-feeding, what was the most important aspect of hygiene – all of which they could now discuss with an Italian-speaking doctor. Infant diseases that are extinct today were rife in the overcrowded, unsanitary conditions then prevailing in the Italian quarter. What a relief to be able to talk about your family's problems in your own language.

The Second World War and after

WW II affected Italians everywhere in Britain even more profoundly than WW I, and the Quarter was no exception. This time, Italy entered the war on the side of the Germans. Most Italian men in the Quarter were rounded up to be sent to internment camps (pp 100, 108) or even imprisoned if suspected of having Fascist sympathies. Some families were parted from their menfolk for as much as 6 years. Some of the men had become naturalised or were regarded as British and conscripted into the British army. One or two, unwilling to take up arms against

The Coach and Horses in the 1920s. It later expanded to take over the newsagents next door.

their own countrymen, declared themselves conscientious objectors (p 145).

Then, during the 1950s and 1960s the Italian character of the *Quartiere* faded. Today only the Church, Lou Resteghini's Coach & Horses, the Gunmakers Arms and Chiappa the Organ Makers remain of the days when the Italian Quarter echoed to the sounds of the varied dialects, the cries of the *bambini*, football matches in the street, the chattering of the *Mammas* and the strident shouts of the vendors. But the Procession in the middle of July continues.

Podesta, Milordini, Dondi and Pozzilli families

The Gunmakers' Arms, Eyre Street Hill

Italian street musicians, 1876

Sometime around 1850 Bartolomeo Podesta, the son of a farm worker, left his home in Genoa, leaving behind his wife and daughter. His wife Felicia was expecting their second child. He set off on the journey to England, making his way through France where he took a boat that landed at London Bridge, finally arriving in Clerkenwell, where he found lodgings in Summer Street. He made a living as an organ grinder, but after a year he realised there was an easier and more lucrative way of earning a living. He began to take in young boys as lodgers, saw that that were fed, then sent them out playing the barrel-organ or other instruments, becoming their *padrone*. The youngsters called him Barbarossa because he sported a very large red beard. By the year 1862 he had made enough money to send to Italy for his wife and two children to come to England. He had of course never seen his son Giovanni – it must have been a joyous meeting. The family remained in the house in Summer Street. Felicia gave birth to four babies during this period, two boys and two girls, but as was commonplace at the time, three of the children died in infancy. The only one to survive was Palmira, born in 1867. Some time during this period Bartolomeo found work as an asphalter, and once actually worked on the roof of the notorious Coldbath Fields Prison. As the years went on his eldest daughter sailed on a ship to South America. She intended to return, but wrote to her parents saying that the journey was so long and frightening that she would never return.

Giovanni grew into a tough, strong young man. He became a cabinet-maker and lived in No.14 Back Hill. He apparently enjoyed a fight; one story had it that when two Irishmen challenged him he came to meet them armed with an axe and, when the men saw him wielding it, they took flight. On another occasion an argument started in a beerhouse in Eyre Street Hill. A fight ensued which continued down into Warner Street, where the two men pulled out knives and stabbed each other. Giovanni left the other man lying in the road and went home to dress his wounds. He remained a bachelor all his short life. He died of tuberculosis in the house in Back Hill at the age of 39.

The second daughter, Palmira, married Oliviero Milordini who was born in Parma in 1869. He was an orphan and at the age of 12 years he walked all the way to England in the company of two brothers, Joseph and Michele Croci. Oliviero was one of the unfortunates who got into the hands of a bad *padrone* for whom he worked selling ice cream in the summer and chestnuts in the winter, sleeping rough because this unscrupulous man was taking so much of the money he earned that he had no money for lodgings. He eventually broke free from this man and later met Palmira Podesta. They fell in love and were married in St Peter's Italian Church in 1885. Their home was No.1 Back Hill; they bought a little shop on the corner of Eyre Street Hill and Warner Street where they sold Italian produce. In 1902 they bought the beerhouse in Eyre Street Hill, The Gunmakers' Arms. They had four children: first Joseph (1886) – his father put him into the black cab business, and at one time he was running 12 cabs, but was put out of business by poor management; then Amadeo (1889), who became a mosaic worker. Their daughter Letizia was born in 1891. Letizia married Luigi Dondi when she was 20 and Oliviero gave the young couple the public house, which then became known as Letty's Cave because of its low ceilings. In 1915 they moved the pub across the road, where it remains to this day. Letizia was left a widow when Luigi died, but she continued to run the pub. The baby of the family, Maria, grew up to marry Alberto Pozzilli.

Bartolomeo (Barbarossa) died aged 74 at his home No.1 Little Bath Street. Felicia went back to The Gunmakers to live with her daughter, where she died aged 90. Oliviero Milordini moved out of the Quarter and retired to Hackney Marshes, where he had bought a pig farm and where he lived until the age of 82. Palmira stayed with her son Joseph until her death in 1956.

Alberto Pozzilli was from Piacenza and came to England when he was 16 years old, to work in a relative's shop. He was called back to Italy to serve in the World War I, but failed his medical because of varicose veins. On his return to England, he moved into lodgings in No.11 Coldbath Square. He met his wife Maria in The Gunmakers' Arms, where she was working with her sister Letizia, and the couple married 6 months later. They moved out of the Quarter for a short time, but Maria wished to return to the Hill, so their next stop was No.11 Eyre Street Hill. Alberto tried several other jobs, but finally joined the mosaic trade. Maria gave birth to two of her sons at No.11. They later moved into improved accommodation in Cavendish Mansions, Clerkenwell Road, where they had to pay £5 key money. Their last son, Alberto Felici, was born in the Mansions in 1926. The three boys attended St Peter's Italian School. In 1932 the family moved out of the Quarter.

Luigi and Letizia Dondi in front of the Gunmakers' Arms, frequently afterwards referred to as "Dondi's"

Cattini and Viazzani families (the story told by Antonietta Viazzani, née Cattini)

A Man of Property

The Cattini and Viazzani families outside the City Arms

Adelaide and her husband Andrea Cattini came from Brato, near Pontremoli in Tuscany. They emigrated to England and in 1881 we find them living above a public house called 'The City Arms', on the corner of Leicester Place and Little Saffron Hill. They ran the pub and also raised four daughters – Assunta, Virginia, Angiolina, and Clementina – and two sons, Arcangelo and Michele. Spare rooms in the pub had to be let out to lodgers. The rooms were divided into sections which were curtained off, each containing a bed, a washbowl and a chamber pot, the object being to cram in as many men as possible. The beds were kept spotlessly clean by Adelaide, and no doubt her daughters as they grew up. The owner of the building housing The City Arms was Luigi Viazzani, who hailed from Cacrovoli, a tiny village on the fringe of Bardi in the province of Parma. Luigi, it would seem, was a man of property, one of the early entrepreneurs, and reputed to be very rich. He not only owned properties in and around Saffron Hill, but also in Mayfair. He also took on the role of banker for other family members. This meant that he kept their money in a safe in one of the rooms in Leicester Place. He never kept records of how much belonged to whom, the consequence being that, when he died, a firm of solicitors known as Binds and

31

Binds simply shared out the money with his next of kin, those who were the closest getting the most. You can imagine the fury within the family whose money he'd been keeping, when they found they were allowed less than others who hadn't left any money at all with him.

One of the lodgers in the rooms over the pub was a nephew of Luigi, Angelo Viazzani. His parents were Antonio (Luigi's brother) and Antonia. Angelo was a piano maker by trade. Music and musical instruments played a large part in the Viazzani family. Assunta Cattini fell in love with the young Angelo and in 1902 the pair were married in St Peter's Italian Church. The happy couple lived in the rooms over the pub and on 17 July 1903 Assunta presented Angelo with their first-born, a girl, Antonietta. Giacomo arrived in 1905, Luigi (Gino) in 1909, followed by twins, Maria and Tonino, in 1912. Antonietta, whose story we follow from here on, remembers her childhood, living over the public house in Little Saffron Hill. She recalls skating down the hill with her friend Lucy Repetati. Lucy lived next door to The City Arms at No.4. They attended St Peter's School, which was immediately opposite their homes. In the school photograph of 1911 Antonietta is standing in the third row, third from the right. She couldn't remember the teacher's name, but said that, although she was very strict, she liked her. During this period Antonietta went back and

The Viazzani family in the 1910s. Seated: Antonia, Antonio, Assunta Cattini. Standing: Ernesto (with riding crop), Antonietta, Rosa Maria, Tonino, Luigi, Angelo and Giacomo

forth to Cacrovoli to stay with her *Nonna*, Antonia Viazzani, who doted on her because she had never had a daughter of her own. Antonietta said that "as soon as she got settled down with her *Nonna*, her mother would send for her to come back to the Quarter, because she missed her so much".

Assunta and Angelo Viazzani returned to Italy in 1914 because Angelo was required to join the Italian Army. WWI had begun. Antonietta remembered looking after her young brothers when her mother went to the station at Fidenza to see her husband off to join his unit at the front.

Members of the Viazzani family spent years to-ing and fro-ing between Italy and England; there never was any great shortage of money. They were all hard-working and a good deal of the money earned abroad was probably ploughed back into the family home in Cacrovoli, Bardi, which was impressively large, so big in fact that the locals named it '*Il Palazzo*'. The house had been built in 1910 by Antonio and Luigi. It was surrounded by a farm and acres of land.

In the early 1920s when Antonietta was 18, her mother broke the news to her that there was to be an addition to the family, and in 1921 baby Andrea arrived, the only one of Assunta's children to be born in Italy.

It was around this time that Antonietta caused havoc within the family by falling in love with one of her uncles who had recently returned from England. Ernesto Viazzani was an asphalter who had been working in London. One of his jobs had been in St Pancras Station. He appreciated the beauty of the architecture and was always extremely proud of saying that he had carried out work there. Can

'Il Palazzo', built by Antonio and Luigi Viazzani, 1910

you imagine the rumpus when the couple stated their intention of marrying? The family protested vehemently, but the couple dug their heels in and somehow a dispensation was obtained from the Pope so they could have their way. Antonietta was 21 and Ernesto 40 years old when they finally married in the church in Bardi. They never regretted their decision and the marriage turned out well. She told me that her wedding day was the happiest day of her life. "Were there many people there?" I asked. "Oh, yes," she said, "Many, many people." "Why do you think that was?" "They all came to see the wedding because my husband came from England!"

Assunta, who had been born amid the hustle and bustle of Clerkenwell, hated the work on the land and never really settled down to life on the farm. Eventually in 1926 a compromise was made: her husband Angelo brought her and the younger children back to Britain, not to London, but to Wales, Port Talbot/Aberavon, where they joined other families from Bardi who had settled there and prospered. It wasn't long before Assunta had sent for Antonietta and Ernesto to join them, to help in setting up a small business, a general store. Antonietta's first son, Valentino, was born during this period. 1930 found this much-travelled couple back in Cacrovoli, living in the big house. Ernesto worked hard on the farm and proceeded to buy the vineyards and woodland surrounding their property. Antonietta was relatively happy; she gave birth to a second son Vittorino, the farm was prosperous, and life was good, but visits from relatives living in London always

33

unsettled her. Almost a decade had passed when the threat of WW II and the uncertainty of Italy's role in it became a source of constant fear for all the families, particularly those with relatives in England. When the inevitable happened and Italy entered the war on the side of the Germans, the Viazzani family, like many others, were in the unhappy position of dealing with the German army on their land. At the same time in England, Antonietta's father Angelo and his youngest son Andrea were interned on the Isle of Man as Italian Nationals. Ironically, another son called Tonino was serving in the British Army.

Although Bardi was only a small town in the mountains, it saw its share of bombs. The American Air Force was constantly trying to blow up a bridge situated just below the town, "*Il Ponte della Baracca*" – unsuccessfully, I was told.

Following the Italian Armistice of 1943, in the light of the imminent arrival of the Germans in the town, Antonietta became fearful for the safety of her eldest son Valentino, who although just a teenager was a well-developed lad and appeared older than his years – the worry being that the Germans might take him to be a partisan, and consequently shoot him. There was a house down in the village that had an outhouse with a large cellar, and it was here that Valentino and some of the other young boys were hidden, the door of the cellar covered with bales of hay. There they stayed until the Germans left the town. As it turned out this was a wise move, because the Germans picked on '*Il Palazzo*' to use as their headquarters.

Antonietta did not return to London until after the war, this time not to Clerkenwell but to Soho, where there was a fast-growing Italian community. The Viazzani family, however, did not forsake the Italian Quarter: Antonietta's grandchildren, Romano and Alma, have always supported St Peter's Italian Church. Alma works hard on the committee of the '*Val Ceno Association.*' She has walked in the processions, and is still seen on Procession Sundays, beavering away at the *Sagra* on the *Val Ceno* stall.

Romano Viazzani is a brilliant musician and is well known in the Italian community as the leader and arranger for the wonderful *L'Orchestra RaRa*. He was responsible at a very young age for the music for many important banquets and weddings held in prestigious venues such as the Hilton, the Grosvenor, and the Café Royal. In 2007 he released three solo albums: *Piazzola – Angel Suite*, *Bobic – Liturgical Suite*, *Viazzani takes Stock* and *Encore*. At the time of writing (2010) he was arranging music for Paul Hutchinson's forthcoming accordion album and writing the music for a new music drama called *The Accordionist* for which he will play the character on a London stage as well as play the music. He adjudicates in competitions all over the UK and Europe and for examinations at the Royal Academy of Music, London.

He is at the top of his game – not bad for an Anglo-Italian whose roots are not only in Bardi, but way back in Clerkenwell's 'Little Italy'.

Six-Fingered Jack
(Antonio d'Ambrosio)
as told to Achille Pompa

Achille Pompa was secretary to London's first Ice Cream Association founded in 1918, and he was also a regular contributor to Backhill Magazine. In September 1919 Antonio D'Ambrosio of Deptford, better known as "Six-Fingered Jack" because of the 12 fingers he had on his hands, and also remembered on account of his deep red complexion, recounted his life story to Achille Pompa.

Antonio was born in Ciacca, a small hamlet in Picinisco, not far from Cassino. At the age of 13, in 1868, he accompanied his two uncles, Davide and Carmine, to Civitavecchia, walking all the way, day and night, carrying their musical instruments, a set of bagpipes (*zampogne*), and *pifferi* (flageolets). They took a cheap passage on a boat to France, where they continued their journey on foot to Dunkirk, thence to London Bridge, where they found a *locanda* (lodging house-cum-restaurant). The landlord, Donato, supplied them with large plates of *maccheroni*. They lodged there for two nights, then continued their journey to Leicester, Bristol and other cities, busking on their way, earning a shilling by whatever means they could find. They returned to Italy in time for the harvesting, again making the journey on foot. They worked on the harvest for 14 days and nights! Antonio's share of the profits was 150 lire (£6). With the 'Bersaglieri' who later became block-ice magnates of Little Italy (Angelo and Bernardo di Felice and Pasquale Riozzi), they attempted the journey to England for a second time, only to find when they reached Paris that, because of the outbreak of the Franco-Prussian War (1870), it was surrounded by German troops. They were arrested as spies and flung into the terrible Val-de-Grâce Prison where they were held for several weeks. They returned to Picinisco with only 50 lire (£2) in their pockets.

Three years later, undeterred, Antonio returned to England. His companions this time were Annuncio Demarco, Crescenzio Cascarni, and Michele di Felice ('*La Gatta*' the cat). They lodged for two years in Eyre Street Hill, he then hired a barrel-organ and tramped the streets of several other cities, finally making enough money to return to his native village with 25 gold sovereigns (roughly 100 *ducati*). Hard-working and determined as ever, he returned to London once more, this time in the company of an uncle Giovanni D'Ambrosio and his children, staying on his own for 5 months and earning an average of 16 shillings a day. Later with his two brothers he purchased a *locanda*. The partnership was short-lived on account of the many arguments that ensued, so they decided to separate in order to remain friends. He returned once more to his homeland but this time the journey was no hardship – he travelled by train! He stopped off in Cassino where he met his wife-to-be. With all this travelling behind him, he was still only 26 years of age. He returned to Clerkenwell,with his wife, where the couple lived in Eyre Street Hill. Behind him were the days of tramping about, soaked by the rain, no boots, only Roman or Etruscan sandals, no umbrella or mackintosh, dried by the sun, playing and begging. Peace at last, with an ice cream barrow! He recalled the noise in 'Little Italy' when the cardless game *mora* was played, the cheapest game in history! Players slammed down one hand on the table, showing any number of fingers, or none, while their opponent shouted out a number from 0 to 5. The noise of fists banging on bare wooden tables was tremendous.

Mora is a very ancient game: under Roman Law, incorrigible gamblers would suffer exile from Rome and the Empire simply for playing it. Antonio never liked the custom among emigrants from certain areas of opening a clasp-knife and sticking the blade in the table before playing, as if to warn your opponent: 'No monkey business!'

Mazza family

In the year 1909 Emilio Mazza from Gropporello, Piacenza, Northern Italy, married Maria Mussi who came from Egola, Pellegrino, Parma. The marriage took place at St Peter's Italian Church, Clerkenwell Road, London, England.

They lived together in harmony in Clerkenwell's Italian Quarter and raised their family there: Ida born in 1910, Antonio 1912, Dina 1914, Noemia 1917 and finally Marina in 1923.

In 1928 they bought the well-known 'Fratellanza Club' on the corner of Warner Street and Great Bath Street, living in the rooms above the club. Many of the men from the Hill spent quite a bit of time there. Bad characters were not encouraged; a gentle word from the owner would send them on their way. There was, however, one infamous incident where one of the Cortesi Brothers took a shot at Darby Sabini, who was saved by a young woman who threw herself in front of him. In court, Louisa Doralli was commended by the judge for her action.

Emilio and Maria returned to Italy in 1939 leaving the children, who were now grown up and working in London. While they were in Italy, the couple helped many escaped prisoners of war who were trying to get home; here is a letter from one of them, Lieutenant E Gazeley of the Royal Artillery:

I was a prisoner-of-war in a camp just north of Parma, but succeeded in escaping on the morning after the Armistice and hearing that allied landings had been made at La Spezia, made my way with 2 of my brother officers towards Varsi. On route, however, my feet became badly blistered, so that I was walking in my socks when I reached Pellegrino and your father's house. This was on September 15th and I stayed with him for 3 days. He was in good health and his hospitality to all the ex-POWs coming through was enormous. He did, however, feel somewhat lonely since his wife had died and his one wish was to get back to England and his family.

I sincerely trust you will see your father shortly.
E Gazeley Lt. R.A.

The Assirati family

Giuseppe Longini Rocco Assirati's story
(as told to "Backhill")

My father Bartolomeo Assirati was born in Casanova, in the province of Bardi, in 1854. He married my mother, Albina Alborini, in 1875. Two years later they emigrated to England where they found a home at No.23 Eyre Street Hill.

I was born amidst squalor and slums in Clerkenwell. Eyre Street Hill consisted of a lot of tumbledown dwellings, choked with humans of the poverty-stricken, peasant class, from all parts of Italy, who had come to London, the supposed Eldorado of the world.

In a small room at No.23 dwelt five human beings, comprising husband, wife and children. The larder is scanty, the floorboards are bare and the fire in the grate is low, for coal costs money and that is scarce. The bitter March winds are penetrating this ramshackle house while the mother offers up an Ave Maria during her labour struggles, for she is assisting me into the world. I arrive in the early hours of the morning of 15 March 1883. Just another mouth to feed: "'Eh, l'amore di Dio non fa niente". It is all excitement in that home for the next few days. "Che bel bambino" says a neighbour as she enters the room and a little gift is given to the mother.

The Northern Italian peasant woman is the embodiment of all that is human in motherhood. Great women, splendid mothers. Fortunate am I to be born of such women. My father was a typical son of the Italian soil, illiterate but intelligent, conditioned to raise and lead a family into the 1880s, a law-abiding man, honest of purpose, an agnostic in religious affairs and, though he never spoke of politics, somewhat conservative in his outlook. Unlike my mother, who held strong religious views and believed in God, yet was of a passionate, rebellious nature, strong in mind and body – a powerful personality who could both love and hate. Well known amongst the Italian community and known by her Christian name, Albina.

So I was the son of Albina – the ninth child of a family of eighteen, only six of whom survived to maturity. The rest succumbed in early childhood to slum diseases – scarlet fever, pneumonia, measles and other complaints caused by the conditions over which my parents had no control.

There were no more reliable and harder workers than these Italian peasants. At the age of nine I was earning my bread and butter and assisting my parents to overcome the economic struggle; yet life was sweet and I was blessed with imagination; I knew of no other world…and I had my mother.

My early schooldays

Holy Family School was situated at the extreme end of Great Saffron Hill adjoining Charterhouse Street, Holborn. An old building, dark and dismal, quite different from the schools of today, but to my young mind it was the Universe itself, the one important place outside my home. Its pupils were mainly London-born Irish and English Catholics. My brothers and I were the only Italians attending the school. Here I was taken at the age of five, the Sisters of Mercy were my teachers until I reached the Higher Standards, where we were taught by men. The Headmaster was an Irishman, very strict, and the boys were often punished for not being able to master their lessons; thus, fear often encouraged us to concentrate on learning. Many poor children attended the school and the great event of the day was a slice of bread and treacle with a cup of cocoa, which was given by a charity.

Scripture played an all-important part in our learning, as in all Catholic schools. My school career was short and I started work at the age of 11: by then I had learned to read and write and this had opened up our eyes to the world in map form. At school I had gained a notoriety for fighting and was looked on as the champion in the class: a fight after school was a common occurrence. That early tuition in the art of self-defence was lasting, and boxing has always remained my favourite sport.

Starting off for school on a cold winter's morning I would see the homeless on doorsteps, mostly old people with their bundles of utensils. My little heart ached for them.

My early youth

The ambition of every thoughtful schoolboy is to assist his mother by starting work, so when my mother bribed the 'school-board' man £1 so that I could leave school I was delighted. I left my school days behind and looked for work. I boldly walked into a shop where 'Boy Wanted' was displayed. "Have you left school?" asked the shopkeeper, I answer "Yes". "How old are you?" Boldly, I reply "13". Thus I became a salesman of toys and trinkets on a stall outside a shop in Exmouth Street, a market just off Farringdon Road. I started work at 8 am and finished at 8 pm. On Saturdays I finished at midnight and received a large cup of cocoa and two thick slices of bread and marmalade, payment for overtime. When I received my first week's wages, I walked home full of pride with the magnificent sum of 5 shillings, which I proudly handed to my mother. In return I was given sixpence, which was a huge sum to a poor boy in those times.

Six months later, anxious to improve my conditions, I changed my job and obtained work with an Italian firm of barrel-organ manufacturers. The other workers were from Southern Italy and only spoke Italian, but in a totally different dialect from that of my parents. As I was a sensitive boy, I was unhappy, so my mother advised me to leave. My next job was dragging a hand barrow all over

Assirati family

London. I am still only 12 years old, but I am learning quickly from the hard school of life, so I drift on. My mother finds me a new job, working for a Swiss German, who ran a business importing live quails from Egypt in late spring and again in early Autumn. The birds were stacked in cages, one hundred birds in each cage, sometimes totalling 6000, contained in a large warehouse near Smithfield – large rooms with whitewashed windows, always closed, which created a very warm, stuffy atmosphere with a peculiar smell caused by the breath and dung of thousands of tiny birds and the breeding of bugs and fleas in countless numbers. Here I am made foreman over three other boys. I am not yet 13, but I am doing a man's job and earning 13 shillings a week, unknown in those days for a boy of that age. I am important to my boss and important to my mother, earning such princely wages.

At the age of 15 I decided to join the Navy. I presented myself to the Naval Recruiting Office in Spring Gardens, close to the Admiralty. At the door I am accosted by a burly sailor, who says: "Where are you from, Jamaica?" I reply: "No, King's Cross". I had a stiff medical inspection and was declared fit and asked if I was ready to 'fight the Russians'. I replied, "Yes". I was booked for the training ship *Impregnable* stationed in Devonport, then handed my papers and told to go home and get my father to sign them. I went home full of pride yet sad at the thought of leaving home. Much consternation: my mother crying at the thought of losing me, but finally, as I am determined, my father agrees to sign. However, the following morning I am doomed to disappointment – my father retracts, under pressure from my mother and brothers. So ended my naval career before it was born.

Aged 17, I went to work for Carlo Gatti on the ice vans. The work was extremely hard. We loaded and unloaded huge blocks of ice, working during the summer from 4.30 am until 6.00 pm. I thrived on the hard work. We were proud of our horses, one in particular that I called 'Napoleon'. Most of my fellow workers were from Northern Italy, healthy, powerful men, full of vitality.

Employees of Carlo Gatti, ice importer

Here is a brief account of Giuseppe's brothers, provided by his son Joe (see below):

Federico Assirati (1881) known to his friends as Fred, was a talented linguist. In the early days he worked for the GPO as a sorter. With the advent of the WW I, his linguistic abilities brought him to the attention of Sir Robert Bruce, Controller at the Post Office Headquarters. As a result he was transferred to the Courier Service. He made numerous trips to Holland with despatches to our Ambassador in the Hague. Once he was torpedoed and on another occasion the mail boat struck a mine; on each of these events he spent many hours in the sea. Among the many decorations for his wartime services he received the OBE for his work in the British Secret Service, and the Cross of Leopold from the Belgian Government.

Daniele Assirati (1885) was the father of Bert Assirati who became a famous professional wrestler and strong man. He was British Heavyweight Wrestling Champion and remained undefeated for 35 years. During this period he also won the World and European Championships.

Giorgio Assirati (1887) (George) was an officer in the British Navy, serving 21 years. He volunteered to return to the service when the 1939-45 war broke out. He died when HMS *Hood* sank with over 1,000 aboard: only 4 men survived.

Giuseppe's son Giuseppe, known to all as Joe Assirati, was born 1905. Here is his story, sent to "Backhill" by a colleague:

Joe's father, Giuseppe, was a boxing instructor, all-round athlete, the possessor of a grand singing voice, and his mother combined all that is best in English womanhood. Joe's boyhood with his two brothers and a sister was as happy as real family life should be. As a boy Joe won a number of boxing contests. He started his first job in the Post Office as a messenger. Aged 16, he had to be vetted by the staff branch and was told that he was too small for continued employment. He was given 6 months to meet the requirements. This was a turning point in Joe's life. He took the Sandow Intensive Physical Culture course, where he studied several methods of physical training, and succeeded in meeting the requirements. Joe was happy to share his knowledge and by the age of 17 he was training other messengers. He was loved and respected by his fellow workers. He was instrumental in 1931 in getting a gymnasium set up for the workers. He was an expert in muscle control.

During WW II Joe was put into the elite Army Physical Training Corps. Back in Civvy Street in 1946, he returned to Mount Pleasant, where he continued to encourage physical fitness among his fellow workers; alas, the rooms that accommodated the hard-won gymnasium and all the equipment had been destroyed by bombing. Joe put tremendous effort in and they managed to pick up the traces. One of the men Joe encouraged with weight-lifting, Carl Goring, won fame for himself and prestige for Mount Pleasant when he won a gold medal in the Empire Games at Perth. He freely acknowledges how much he owed to Joe for his instruction and encouragement. Joe retired from the Post Office in 1965.

The Sesti and Roberto families

An example of the integration of the Italians and the Irish in 1870

Family history told to Olive Besagni in October 1995 by Umberto Roberto (Bert)

Sesti family

Mary Ann Finn, a young Irish girl, fell in love with an Italian boy, Pancrazio Sesti, a young Italian immigrant who hailed from Chiesina Uzzanesi, Lucca, in the province of Tuscany. The couple were married in 1877 and within six years they had five children. They were contented and happy; they were living in the Italian Quarter amongst immigrants like themselves, and were as happy as any couple could be, albeit in not the most salubrious conditions. Then fate dealt the young couple a terrible blow. Pancrazio was taken ill. Tuberculosis! – common enough in those times, the worst news the doctor could impart – must have shattered the young woman. Her husband's only chance of survival was to return to Italy, Chiesina Uzzanesi, where the fresh mountain air would give him a better chance of beating the disease. How could Mary Ann cope with five young children, let alone keep a roof over their heads? But there was no option, Pancrazio had to go. Mary Ann was to remain in London and continue with her work as an embroiderer; the money was needed to feed and clothe the children. After a lot of heart searching, Mary Ann agreed to let her two older daughters, 5-year-old Winnie and 7-year-old Rosa, go to Italy with their father, where at least they would be fed and looked after by the Sesti family.

Pancrazio set off with his two little daughters on the arduous journey back to his village. What a sorrowful parting it must have been. Little did they know that worse was to come. How Mary Ann survived that terrible year is beyond our comprehension. First the baby, Frank, died aged one year. Then little Nellie Sesti, only 3 years old, was to begin her first day at St Peter's Italian School. The excited little girl set off, when suddenly her hat blew off. She darted into the road after the precious hat and was knocked down and fatally injured by a horse-drawn tram. As if that wasn't enough, news came from Italy that Pancrazio had taken a turn for the worse and died – three deaths within a year. What a desperate situation that poor 27-year-old woman was in; she was left just with John, now 9 years old. She had to work until she had enough money to go to Italy and bring her daughters home. Ten years elapsed before Mary Ann had managed to scrape together enough money to make the long journey to the province of Lucca and bring her girls home. What must her feelings have been when, after the joy of their reunion, she found that she couldn't talk to them! The girls had forgotten their native tongue and Mary Ann couldn't speak Italian. It didn't help matters when Rosa, the eldest girl, made it clear that she didn't want to return to England with her mother and

Winnie. She never set foot in England again: she remained in Italy and eventually married a young man from Pistoia, living in Lucca until she died at the age of 90. John too went abroad, this time to the USA, when he was 16 and never returned. He changed his name to Finn and lost contact with his family back in London.

In 1905, Mary Ann returned to Clerkenwell with 15-year-old Winnie. They found a flat in Skipwith Buildings on the Bourne Estate on the corner of Clerkenwell Road and Leather Lane, where a mixture of English and Irish families lived; their neighbours were people like themselves. After the freedom and fresh air of the Italian mountainside, they may not have felt that an inside tap and a lavatory with a chain made up for the grime and dirt of London (plumbing in Italian villages at that time was non-existent).

The flats were just across the road from St Peter's Italian Church and 'The Hill'. Bright youngster that she was, the little Irish/Italian girl soon picked up her English language again and was soon able to communicate with the other young-sters, girls and boys like herself. She went to the church regularly and was soon join-ing in with the social activities, the *Children of Mary*, and dances, in the School Hall.

Winnie was proficient in the Italian language and in Italian cuisine. She was also very pretty. It wasn't very long before she met her fate in one Raffaele Roberto.

Roberto family

Michele Roberto was born in Nola, 15 miles from Naples in Southern Italy. In the year 1856, aged 21, he married Teresa Scognamiglio, a local girl. The couple had four children, including three daughters, Assunta, Attilia, and Margherita. It is their son Raffaele, born in 1884, whose life we are concerned with. Shortly after the birth of Margherita in 1887 Michele left his family and went to England. He was fortunate to have a trade: he was a skilled tinsmith and was employed in the making of equipment for distilleries. He set off on the long journey, working his way across France to this final destination, Clerkenwell, London. He tried various ways of making money then realised that one of the primary sources of income for the Italian immigrants was the making and selling of ice cream. As a tinsmith he quickly got the idea of making ice-cream freezers; by 1894 he had an established business. He sent for his wife and children. Once the family had been reunited, Raffaele, now aged 10, and his two young sisters started to receive their education at St Peter's Italian School. Soon another two babies came along: Umbertino born in 'The Italian Quarter' in 1897 and finally, in 1899, Rosa, the baby.

The family settled down in Clerkenwell with occasional trips to Nola. When Umbertino was 14, his mother took him with his sister Margherita to visit their relatives there, but the journey was ill-fated. Umbertino caught typhoid and died after a short illness. Back in England Michele was angry: there was an epidemic in Nola at that time and he felt that if only they had stayed at home in London he would still have his son. Teresa, grieving for her child, remained in Nola with her daughter. With the advent of WW I in 1914, they were unable to return. When the war was over Margherita, by now a young lady, met and married a local boy,

Antonio D'Angelo, and left home. Teresa sent for her youngest daughter Rosa, who left England to live with her mother and never returned.

Here we take up the story of Raffaele. As a youth he assisted his father in the business.

One Sunday morning at St Peter's he met and fell in love with young Winnie Sesti. His father frowned upon the match – after all, she wasn't Italian, was she? However, it wasn't long before Winnie won the family over: she was an excellent cook with an excellent knowledge of Italian cuisine and of the Italian language.

Raffaele Roberto with his horse and cart outside St Pancras station

The marriage took place in the Italian Church in 1905 and they settled in Little Italy. Their first child was a boy, Michele (Michael), then came Teresa (Cissie). Raffaele and Winnie were an adventurous pair: by the year 1910 they were living in New York, where their daughter, Rosa, was born, returning two years later to Nola, where another boy, Umberto (Bert), arrived. He was the only one of their children to be born in the home country.

Back in Clerkenwell where they set up home in Lloyd's Row, a small turning between St John Street and Rosebery Avenue. It was from here that Raffaele ran his business as a horse-and-cart contractor.

The horses were housed in a nearby mews in Finsbury. The horses and carts would be hired for removals and daily business needs by traders such as ice-men, bakers and milkmen. The family was making a good living. The family again increased during this period: Giovanni (John), and Raffaele junior were born. Meanwhile, Grandfather Michele, who was known to his grandchildren as 'Papa Gros', was still carrying on with his original trade, supplying the ice-cream vendors. In 1917 at the age of 60, he suffered a fatal stroke. Grandmother Teresa (*Mamma Gros*) was unable to attend her husband's funeral because WWI was still raging, and to travel to England would have been too risky. She never returned to England, but Raffaele, her only living son, returned to Nola every year to see his mother. He always went in November and stayed a month to see to her financial needs and well-being.

With the demise of *Papa Gros* in 1917 the Italians in the ice-cream trade missed Michele (*Papa Gros*), the source from which they hired their freezers and other tin goods. They appealed to Raffaele to resume *Papa Gros*'s business, as they were suffering from the lack of equipment. Raffaele, whose business acumen left

Raffaele Roberto trading ice cream freezer barrels on Eyre Street Hill

nothing to be desired, had already realised that with the advent of the motor car his horses and carts would be unable to compete. He decided to pick up where *Papa Gros* had left off and sold the transport business.

The family moved into No.4 Little Bath Street where the couple settled long enough to add one more child to their family, Dante, who arrived in 1922. In all there were seven surviving children.

Having taken up his father's trade, he soon expanded into other sectors of the ice-cream trade, adding to the freezer tubs and barrels that his father had hired out barrows, wafer biscuits, flavouring and boilers for the milk.

Raffaele's son, Umberto (Bert's) account of his early years living in the Italian Quarter

"They were happy years, very happy years, wonderful times, we never felt threatened, we never went hungry, and we loved our way of life. At home we ate in the Italian tradition, our playground was the streets in the Quarter; most of our friends were from Italian families and we were entirely happy with our situation. After school there were serious games of football or cricket under the bridge in Warner Street with close friends, Tony Della Savina, Lu Terroni, Fred Miserotti and other budding Stanley Matthewses. Our teenage years were spent hanging out with the lads and chatting up the local *signorine* (young girls). Friday night was bath night when the water would be heated in the copper in the scullery and carried indoors in pans to the tin bath in front of the fire – luxury!"

Others of Bert's generation tell the same story. Men and women who were born within the confines of the Hill or lived their formative years there look back with few regrets about their childhood circumstances; the lack of material things was of no consequence to these children.

The entrepreneur

The year is 1926, Bert is 14 years old, and it's time to go out into the world and earn a living. His first job was that of office boy with a company in Red Lion Street, 'Radio Vacuum Cleaners', importers of vacuum cleaners from America. Bert got bored with the job after 6 months. Then without a word to anyone he took one of the cleaners out. He identified a likely-looking house, knocked on the door and, when the housewife opened the door, he threw a handful of confetti into the hall, then proceeded to demonstrate the efficiency of the cleaner. The surprised housewife immediately bought the cleaner for £20. Bert took the money back to his boss and asked if he could go out on the road as a rep. He earned £1 for every cleaner that he sold. The money was good, bearing in mind that Bert was only 16 years old. The cleaners were not the end of the line for

Umberto (Bert) Roberto and Anna Manzi before their wedding in St Peter's Italian Church on 4 June 1939, with a reception at Reggiori's famous restaurant at King's Cross (Luigi and Pietro Reggiori were two of the most successful Swiss-Italian immigrants)

Bert and he tried various other ventures, and still helped his father out from time to time. When Bert was 21 he decided to return to Nola, as he wished to improve his Italian, but he found on his arrival that there were many people there who could converse in English; moreover the local dialect wasn't what he was seeking. He made a very shrewd move by joining the Italian Army, where, apparently because he came from England, he was allowed to sign up for just 6 months and also choose where he wished to be stationed. He chose to go to Naples where he served with the *Autocolonna del 10 Centro Automobilistico*, where they made him their *Conduttore* in the *3 Gara di Regolarita' per Autocolonna Militari* and the boy from England came third and had a very nice looking diploma and medal to prove it. He enjoyed the months spent in the army and he achieved his goal of improving his Italian. He was that very rare person, a soldier with money in his pocket. The regulars earned a pittance and most of what they earned was sent to their families. If he lit a cigarette there would be a queue for the dog end. One night he decided to go for a meal to Zia Teresa's, a high-class restaurant in Naples. The waiter noted his uniform and refused to serve him. Bert was furious, he sought out the proprietor and told her he had eaten there before, was he now being refused because he was wearing the Italian Army uniform? After his altercation with the boss, the waiter even dusted the chair before Bert sat down for his meal. After six months he returned to England happy, he could now speak perfect Italian.

Bert's next venture was into the hiring out of 'fruit machines' (one-arm bandits). He enjoyed the work as it entailed plenty of travelling to the coast, where he installed the machines in the arcades of seaside resorts. In winter he would travel to fairgrounds all over the country. It was a lucrative business. In 1938 Bert went to see a Mr Manzi who was also in the machine trade, and it was there he met Anna Manzi; they courted for a year, then married and set up home in Highbury. Apart from the outbreak of WW II, things were going well enough. In 1940 they were blessed with their first-born, a son, Tony.

When Italy entered the war on 10 June 1940, Bert realised that because he was born in Italy, he was a prospective internee: they were picking up Italians everywhere. Sure enough, the call came. Bert bade a sad farewell to his young wife and baby and was sent to the Isle of Man. However, the many friends he made there made life tolerable.

There were bad days after the air-raids, when they waited for news from home, worrying about the safety of loved ones. One of the worst times Bert recalled was the day that two of the boys from "The Hill", Micky and Ben Chiavenga, whose family lived above Mariani's, now Gazzano's Delicatessen in Farringdon Road (p 6), were informed that their mother and two sisters had been killed by a bomb that had landed on Lady Owens's Grammar School, in Owen Street off St John Street. The family were in the shelter under the school, which received a direct hit. Bert remembered with affection a Doctor Borghesi who was the internal medical officer for the camp and whose great compassion and concern for the internees made life bearable on the Island.

Bert's home in Highbury was demolished by a bomb; fortunately his wife, Anna, and baby Tony had been evacuated to the country. After 18 months Bert was released and returned to London to carry on with his life. When the war was over, Anna and the baby returned and set up home temporarily in a flat in Islington Park Street. In 1950 Anna was expecting a baby, but their joy was marred by the discovery that Anna had a serious heart condition. The baby Eugene was a fine boy, but the birth took its toll, and Anna's health was badly impaired. Three years later in May 1953, Anna passed away in The Italian Hospital, Queen Square. Bert was devastated, but at least he had his boys: Tony, now 13 years old, and baby Eugene. His work with the machines entailed travelling all round the country. After a year he decided to end the travelling – it was not good for the boys and he needed time with his children. A friend advised him that the carpet trade was a good bet, so he went for it. He opened a shop on the Old Street roundabout, and it was a successful venture. In 1960, the shop was requisitioned to make way for a larger Old Street roundabout (as it is today). He then bought a large shop in Leather Lane. The carpet shop in Leather Lane was well known and many of his customers were old friends from 'The Hill'. I said to Bert, "You could say that you'd returned to 'The Hill.'" Bert said, "I never left it, I always went to 10 o'clock

Mass at St Peter's Italian Church, where I read the lesson every Sunday for years."

The Roberto carpet business was passed on to Bert's son, Tony, and is now located on Clerkenwell Road in part of the Bourne Estate, where Mary Anne Sesti, Toni's great-grandmother, lived in Skipwith Buildings in 1905.

Michele (Micky), Giovanni (Johnny), Raffaele and Teresa (Cissie) Roberto

Michele (Micky), born in 1905, was the eldest son. Aged 14 he began his working life as a commis waiter in the West End. Most Italian parents considered this to be a good starting point for a career; people would always eat! His training led to a job in a well-known night spot 'The Kit Kat Club' in the Haymarket, just off Piccadilly. Later, having inherited the nomadic tendencies of the family, he became a ship's waiter. He completed several trips on ocean-going liners. One day he jumped ship in New York and stayed there, becoming one of the thousands of illegal immigrants who were slipping into the country. He worked in night-clubs and speakeasies. He married an American girl, Nellie Carifa, whose mother ran a speakeasy. The couple had two daughters, Winnie (named after her grandmother Roberto) and Aileen. They had a successful restaurant in Mulberry Street, New York and things were going well, until, sadly, his wife Nellie died, aged 30. Fortunately Nellie had a sister who stepped in and helped him look after the two little girls. When America entered the war in 1942 the government decreed that, provided they registered, all illegal immigrants would be granted American citizenship. Micky took advantage of this, and what a relief that must have been. In due course he met and married a young Ukrainian girl, Virginia. They moved to Chester in Philadelphia, Pennsylvania, where they built up a successful business, a delicatessen and butcher's shop. They had four children, Winnie the eldest, from his first marriage, grew up to marry a young West Point Officer, an American Italian, who eventually made the rank of 2-Star General. Young Winnie and the General had five daughters and four of them married American Army Officers. Micky spent the rest of his days in Chester where he died in 1991 aged 84. After the fateful day when he jumped ship in New York, Michele was never to set foot on English soil again.

Giovanni (Johnny)

Johnny, son number three, was born in 1915 and grew up in the Italian Quarter. His working life began in 1934 as an apprentice in ladies' hairdressing at Bruno's Salon in Essex Road. In true Roberto fashion he wasn't long in aquiring his own shop. His father set him up with a salon in New Bridge Street, Ludgate Circus. In 1937 he married an English girl who bore him a daughter, Margaret. 1941 saw him conscripted into the British Army as a non-combatant. He was posted as an interpreter in an Italian prisoner-of-war camp in the Midlands. Like so many others in times of war, his wife left him, leaving little Margaret with his mother, Winnie. When the war ended he returned to the Italian Quarter into the bosom of his family.

Leaving the trauma of his wife's desertion behind him, he opted to make a new start and join his brother in America, where, with his newly acquired skills (typing, administration and organisation) gained from the time spent in the POW camp, he would look for employment in the secretarial field. By 1949 he was employed by a woman reputed to be one of the richest in America, whose family were in oil. To give some idea of the status of this family, they entertained, among others, the Duke and Duchess of Windsor.

In 1950 he had bought a flat on 10th Avenue. His father, Raffaele, arrived in New York to help him to prepare for the arrival of his daughter, Margaret, who was to be brought over to the States by her Grandmother Winnie and Uncle Dante. Margaret was happily reunited with her father, Johnny. Dante returned to England, but Winnie and Raffaele stayed on to look after Margaret. However, the sad news from England in 1953, when Bert's wife Anna died so tragically, hastened the death of Raffaele. Apparently he was very fond of her and his health deteriorated, and he died from a heart attack.

After her husband's demise, Winnie, torn between the families in England and the others in New York, set a pattern that she was to follow for many years, dividing her time between New York and London. Ever-ambitious Johnny was now employed by the head of The Chase National Bank. Part of his job was to organise functions for VIPs. He was on first-name terms with many of the old Hollywood stars: Bette Davies, George O'Brien, Betsy Drake (who married Cary Grant) and others. He was head-hunted by Robert Montgomery, a very big name in those days. He took up the offer and was in charge of the star's affairs for many years. He was remarried in 1960 to an American girl, Florence (second time lucky). Eventually he retired to Florida, where home was a country club, where he played golf and enjoyed the climate. Every year in the summer he would return to England for a holiday, where he stayed with his brother Bert at the house in Highbury.

Teresa and Cissie

During the 1930s, Raffaele bought the tobacconist shop in Back Hill which is still there. Cissie, his eldest daughter, worked there for a time until she went to Nola to visit her relatives for a holiday. She took a trip to Rome where she met one Angelo Rossi, a young Roman policeman. They married. Cissie's intention was to return home, but when WW II loomed she decided to stay until the threat passed. Unfortunately, by the time she wanted to return to London, war had become inevitable, and she stayed. Meanwhile her brother, Raffaele (Raffey), who was studying medicine in Naples, needed looking after, so she moved there for a time. When Italy entered the war her husband, Angelo, was called up into the Italian Army. Raffey, who was exempt from the Italian Army because he had a British passport, was drafted to a hospital in Rome as a non-combatant, where he completed his degree, at the same time as caring for war casualties. Cissie's husband was wounded in Tripoli and was sent to the hospital in Rome where Raffey was working as a doctor. Cissie then moved to Rome where she was able to be with her husband and brother. When the war ended, she returned to Clerkenwell with her husband, Angelo, and their two daughters, Tina and Anna.

Doctor Raffaele Roberto (Raffey) also returned to London and applied to the Italian Hospital, Queen Square, but found that his Italian qualifications did not allow him to practise in this country, and had to commence his studies all over again, in order to obtain an English medical degree. He worked in the Italian Hospital until 1950. He got restless and determined to join his parents and brothers in America. When he arrived in New York, he found that his Italian and English qualifications stood for nothing in the United States, so he had to gain a third degree in order to obtain American credentials. In true Roberto fashion he did very well. He climbed the tree, became a physician and surgeon and entered the field of plastic surgery. His final post was with the American Express Company, a job involving (true to his genes and history), travelling world-wide for the company in his capacity as doctor and surgeon.

Dante and Rene Crowley

Dante, the youngest member of the Roberto family, attended St Peter's Italian School. On leaving school, he joined his father and brother in the business of supplying and installing 'fruit machines' at fairgrounds and seaside resorts. The business had a great boost when the Americans entered the war and thousands of American troops landed in England. The family won a contract to supply the one-arm bandits to American air bases and army camps. After the war Dante made several trips to America to see his parents and brother.

One evening a young lady of Irish descent, Irene Crowley, received a phone call from a girl-friend. "Have you got an evening dress?" the friend enquired. "Yes I have" answered Rene, "In that case how would you like to come to a fund-raising ball, at Caxton Hall? The Anglo-Italian Society are putting on a dinner-dance to raise funds for the Italian Hospital, and someone is unable to come. I know it's short notice, but we'd be really pleased if you'd fill the place." Rene went off to the ball and it was there she met young Dante Roberto. They married in 1952.

Rene lived on the Bourne Estate, Clerkenwell Road. Her father, Patrick Crowley, a successful bookmaker, was known to all as Sante Crowley. There is a story concerning the way Sante got his nickname. The Crowley family lived on the same landing as Mary Ann Sesti (Winnie's mother, see above). When the Crowley family were expecting the birth of a new baby, Mary Ann, as friend and neighbour, was waiting to hear the news. On Christmas morning there came a knock on the door and one of the Crowley youngsters was standing there very excited and blurted out "Sante's here, Sante's arrived!" Henceforth Rene's father was known as Sante!

Dante and Rene's marriage was happy one, and another successful Anglo-Irish union was made. They set up home at No. 65 Kelross Road, Highbury. The couple have four sons and a daughter, Raffaele (Rockie), Ricardo (Ricky), Daniela, Giovanni (John), and Paolo (Paul).

Since the children left home, Dante and Rene have retired to a new home.

Onerato Comitti

Glassblowers and craftsmen

Example of an Onerato Comitti clock

Onerato Comitti was one of the more fortunate immigrants. He almost certainly had relatives already here, prosperous families who had arrived during the industrial revolution. These families were from Northern Italy, from Como, where glassblowing was a prominent local industry. Onerato came to England, it is believed from Como, around 1845. At this time barometers were quite rare, glass-blowing was the primary skill needed to create them, and wealthy industrialists were taking an interest in the sciences, all of which resulted in a demand for decorative wall barometers. The Italian craftsmen had no trouble in creating ornate designs that included intricate wood carvings, inlays and marquetry. The barometers soon became a 'must have' in the homes of the Victorian elite. Elaborate clocks were also much sought after.

Sometime in the late 1850s, as business increased, Onerato set up his premises in a row of shops in Mount Pleasant. As the shops had living accommodation above, the rooms were let out to other immigrants; they were very careful about their tenants and chose only those families who came with a recommendation as clean and hard-working people. Many families remembered happy times living in the rooms above Comitti's.

Onerato had a son, Luigi, and a daughter, Bianca. Luigi joined his father in the business and it was he who formed the company 'O. Comitti & Son Limited' in the year 1898. Bianca married an Englishman, George Barker, who worked for the company. When Luigi died, the Barker family carried on the business.

One of the tenants, Maria Di Lucca, who lived in No.53 during the Barker period, told me that he was a very kind man and a good landlord. George's son, Ronald James, married Beryl Raymond; they had seven children: William, Clare, Susan, Thomas, Simon, Jonathan and Angela. These descendants of the Barker family carried on with the business and are still trading today.

Comitti & Son at 51 Mount Pleasant, c.1914

Molinari family

Luisa Molinari busy as usual helping in the Procession

Luisa Molinari was the youngest daughter and only surviving child of Marietta and Taddeo Molinari, a family well known and respected in the Italian community for their involvement with the Italian Church, the choir, the church bazaars and the annual procession. As a family they played a central role in the community and worked hard to keep up the traditions and culture of their home country.

At the time of my meeting with Luisa in 1993 she was about to celebrate her 80th birthday. She was living in a large house in Devonia Road, Islington, sharing with her niece Marie (her older sister Annie's only daughter). Luisa had not been enjoying the best of health for a number of years, but her looks belied her age and her state of health.

The story, as told by Luisa, begins with her father Taddeo, who lived with his parents, two brothers and two sisters in the picturesque little town of Borgo Val

Di Taro, in the province of Parma, Northern Italy, in the late 1800's. They enjoyed a relatively happy life as they owned both their house and their land. Unfortunately his mother died whilst the children were very young. His father did his best to cope with his young family, but eventually remarried. Unlike his first marriage, this was an unhappy union. Taddeo's father decided to seek a new life in South America, leaving his young family with their stepmother, with the intention of sending for them once he was established. Sadly for his children, he contracted yellow fever and died. The stepmother, clearly a poor manager, mortgaged the house and the land, leaving the children destitute.

Taddeo grew up in poverty, but in spite of his adversities he had learnt a rare craft, that of painting church ceilings and applying gold leaf. He resolved to seek his fortune in England. He arrived in the Italian Quarter in 1893 and soon found work decorating the ornate interiors of the music halls and theatres which abounded in London, for example the Gaiety Theatre.

Eventually, having made enough money, he returned to Borgo Val Di Taro, and married his childhood friend Marietta. In 1899 he brought his young wife back to England. They found rooms in Bath Street, where their first baby, Antonio, was born. Marietta soon became disillusioned with the insanitary living conditions, the overcrowding and the constant struggle against the dirt and grime of the large city. Conditions were slightly better in their next home in Gough Street, but by this time she was expecting her second child. Annie's birth left Marietta in poor health and she was homesick. She yearned to return home to Borgo, where she had spent her days in the tranquillity of the local convent where she was taught by the nuns in the art of embroidery, the exquisite work used to enhance the vestments of the priests and the fine linens used in trousseaux.

Taddeo had no choice but to send them back. He remained in London where there was still plenty of work, which enabled him to maintain his family, but in the course of time he began to suffer from lead-poisoning due to the high lead content of the paint he was using, which caused bad attacks of colic. His days as a craftsman were over and he had to choose another trade. The only work he could find was of a menial kind, in the kitchens of the big restaurants and hotels of the West End. In 1904 they were back in Clerkenwell's Italian Quarter where they found a flat above the row of shops owned by Onerato Comitti in Mount Pleasant. They had been recommended to the owner by friends from Borgo who were already living there. The Molinaris' flat was above the Comitti showrooms, and one of the stipulations of the tenancy agreement was that Marietta keep the reception hall and brass stair-rails, etc. in pristine condition, a task she was only too pleased to carry out. She was happy in her new home. They got on well with the other families and lifelong friendships were established with the Servini family, the Menozzis, the Zanellis and others who dwelt above the shops. Two new family members were born, Damaso (Damso) in 1908 and finally Luisa in 1913.

In the years that followed, unable to find any other employment, Taddeo continued to work in the hotel kitchens, more often than not underground, often meant standing on wet floors and sometimes actually in pools of water. The horrendously long and unsocial hours meant that he was unable to spend much time at home with his family. In later years he developed a rheumatic condition which plagued him for the rest of his life. He vowed that his children would receive a good education and never have to work in such conditions

He clearly steered them in the right direction. Antonio (Tony), the eldest, went into banking. He was a dapper figure, immaculately turned out, always carrying a rolled umbrella and sporting an impeccable moustache; he was known

Luisa Molinari (front row, first on left) on a day out with the "Children of Mary"

for his untiring efforts for fundraising and charitable works, and was a greatly respected member of the community.

Annie was a brilliant seamstress and was employed in the finest haute couture houses. She actually made skirts for Queen Elizabeth, the Queen Mother. Luisa, after winning a scholarship, went to Hara House Convent in The East India Dock. By the age of 19 she was employed as a linguistic secretary. Across the years the family spent most of their leisure hours working for their beloved St Peter's Italian church. Marietta and Annie made many of the costumes still to be seen in the annual procession of 'Our Lady of Mount Carmel', whilst Luisa looked after the wardrobe and dressed the participants in the tableaux, and the walkers.

Damso was an accountant, a confirmed bachelor who enjoyed life to the full, to be found most evenings relaxing with his friends in the Coach and Horses, the popular pub in Warner Street, where he was known for his formidable skill as a card player. His contribution to the church began at the age of 9 when he joined the choir; he had been taught tonic solfa by Mr Delaney at the school. He also used to clean the old church organ, and put the music on the stands – no mean task, when you consider that the choir in those days consisted of 40-50 singers. When he was older he not only conducted, but also would fill in for absent altos in a fine falsetto, as well as singing his own part with the tenors.

As it was around Christmas time, I asked Luisa to recount her memories of the festive season as a youngster in the Italian community. Christmas for the young Luisa actually began on 13 December, the celebration for Santa Lucia: she would leave her shoes out and in the morning would find a penny or maybe an orange inside them. On Christmas Eve Taddeo would make a Christmas tree by winding garlands of holly around a double gas mantle. The crib would be set up, and beside the crib they would put a glass of milk for Our Lady, bread and *grasso* (pork fat) and straw for the donkey. Meanwhile Mamma would be making 1000 *agnolini* (small ravioli), a task which probably kept her mixing, rolling and stuffing into the early hours. Apart from these activities there would be the ritual meal of *baccala* (dried cod), *polenta* and *anguilla* (eels) followed by a short walk to St Peter's for Midnight Mass. They would meet a great many of their friends on their walk, all glowing with the anticipation (and no doubt a glass or two of chianti) of the feast of music and the celebration of the Nativity ahead of them. The church would be packed to the doors. On the way home from Mass it was the custom to call into Auntie Angelina's (Bergomini) for a final glass of wine and a liqueur.

Christmas dinner would consist of *antipasto*, followed by *agnolini* in *brodo* (chicken broth), then a fine capon with vegetables etc. Card games would follow. The family were never allowed to leave the house before midnight, after which they would go to relatives or friends, for a good sing-song or a party.

The *grasso* (fat) that had been put by the crib was put away and kept to be used in emergencies as a poultice.

Pinazzi–Mora family

Martino Mora (left) outside his bootmaker's shop with his friend Taddeo Molinari (p 54)

The following story was prompted by a phone-call from the granddaughter of Martino Mora. She told me that her 83-year-old mother, Ida Lucili, née Mora, was so touched when she saw a photo of her late father, Martino Mora, with Taddeo Molinari standing outside Martino's cobbler's shop in Mount Pleasant, that she volunteered to tell me her family story.

In the late 19th century Giuseppina Pinazzi left her home in Borgo Val di Taro, Parma to join her uncle, Antonio Pinazzi, who had settled in the Italian Quarter where he had a small *birra* shop (pub) in Warner Street. Giuseppina, to quote her daughter, "already had Marino in tow at the time."

Unlike the majority of young immigrants Giuseppina was bringing a sum of money with her, 25 *Marenghi* (gold pieces), which she had earned at home knitting for a wealthy family. A message from Martino met her on arrival, that, as she had some money, wouldn't it be a good idea if she sent him the fare so that he could join her. Wisely she refused. Undeterred by his inamorata's refusal, he set off on foot, working his way along the journey.

He finally made it, to find that Giuseppina was doing quite well working for her Uncle Tony, and was leading a relatively comfortable life. Eventually love conquered all and the young couple were married in St Peter's Italian Church on 5 February 1890. Their honeymoon was a trip around Hyde Park in a horse and carriage. Leicester Place, a little courtyard opposite St Peter's School, was their first home. Maria was born in January 1891 and it wasn't long before her mother was expecting again. They then moved to a small house in Warner Street, in a little row near Ben Resteghini's pub, where the Terroni (p 102) also lived. As the family increased in number, so the struggles began. Martino did his best; he had a good trade as a *calzolaio* (boot maker) and Giuseppina did her bit for the family income by sewing, knitting and, at one time, plucking quail. If she made even one small tear in the skin of a bird it would be discarded and she would receive no pay for it. In the 15 years that followed they had another seven children: the second baby, Angiolina, September 1892; Joe, 1894; Luisa, 1896; Luigi, 1898; Ottavio, 1900; Teresa, 1903 and little Ida, 1906, whose short life ended at the age of 2.

These were hard times for the family, but their situation was no worse than that of many of their neighbours and friends. Martino attempted to set up a business with a friend, Bergomini, but the fact was, there weren't enough people in the vicinity who could afford to have shoes made for them. Giuseppina and the children had to make trips to the *Red House* in Clerkenwell Road, a charitable institution, where, after a means-test, they would be issued with bread and the bare necessities. Little Joe would go down to Smithfield Market to collect wood to take home, where he would chop it up and sell it to the neighbours for firewood. One day the family received a letter from Martino's brother, who had emigrated to South Africa, and had found work in the gold mines in the Transvaal. After much deliberation, they decided that Martino should try his luck there. Exactly which year that happened is lost, but he must have returned with some money, because the family were able to afford their next move.

They had found a shop in Yardley Street, a small turning off Rosebery Avenue. There was accommodation over the shop, and Martino started to do shoe repairs as well as make boots. Their quality of life was beginning to improve, when yet another addition to the family, Ida, (named after the little one who had died), arrived in the year 1910. Ida, whose memories we are recalling, would sit on the shop counter watching her father as he worked; the boots were all hand-sewn and he used wooden nails. The pattern for the boot was made by the customer placing his foot on a piece of paper on which Martino would trace the shape of the sole.

In his leisure hours Martino would often take Ida to the Mazzini-Garibaldi Club in Laystall Street, where she would watch him play *bagatelle*, and also she would accompany him to the games of *bocce* played in the clearing behind Dondi's pub, where many hours were spent by the men of the colony.

Finances improved as the older children started work. Maria, Lena and Joey all worked at Comoy's, the pipe factory in Rosebery Avenue. The little shop in Yardley Street was open house to all their friends and relatives from the quarter, who passed by on their way to Exmouth Street Market.

Giuseppina returned to Italy only once, but it was a sad and traumatic journey. She went to bring home her eldest daughter, Maria, who was on holiday in Pontremoli, her husband Giullio's birthplace in Northern Italy, and where she was stricken with a fatal illness. Her mother brought her home, where she died tragically at the early age of 31 years, leaving a young husband and two little daughters, Elena and Olga.

In 1924 the family made their final move, this time nearer to the Hill, to another shop with accommodation above in Mount Pleasant, opposite Comitti's, where their old friends the Molinari family lived, among other friends. Giuseppina was very happy to be reacquainted with her childhood friend, Marietta, and the two families became very close.

In later years, when their financial situation improved, Martino visited his family in Borgo once a year, where he had a brother known as *"Panzon"* (dialect for Poncione, big belly). The young Ida was bemused when she finally made the

Pinazzi-Mora family

50th anniversary of the Mazzini-Garibaldi Club. Front row, second from right, Maestro Ferrari (p 153)

journey to Italy and met Panzon, who, in her words, "was like a shadow, as thin as a rake!". Maybe he had just had a large appetite!

On Christmas Day 1931 Ida married Giulio Lucili, her late sister Maria's husband. She gladly took on the role of mother to her sister's two little girls. I asked Ida if she was happy on her wedding day. She said, "Not really, because it was the day that my father died." It was Martino's wish that the wedding should go ahead because he wanted to see his youngest daughter settled. She also told me that their wedding was the only time that a couple had ever been married in St Peter's Italian Church on Christmas Day. Father Chiapponcelli performed the ceremony.

Menozzi–Zanetti family

Wedding of Lisa Zanetti and Gioacchino Menozzi, 1922

Giuseppina Delmistro married Dimitrio Zanetti (a mosaic worker) in the village of Maniago, in the Friuli region, Northern Italy, in 1900. Like many others before them, the couple travelled to England on foot. It is not clear how long the journey took them, but 1903 found them in the Italian Quarter, living at No.8 Mount Pleasant, where the couple spent the rest of their lives. Their daughter Elisa (Lisa) was born in the first year, followed by baby Tilli, then Vittorio (Victor) in 1906 and Antonio (Tony) in 1908.

When Lisa was 18 she married Gioacchino Menozzi, who hailed from Bardi (Parma). The groom was a tall, handsome, likeable young man, well thought of by all who knew him. The wedding was in St Peter's Italian Church in 1921 and Lisa made her own wedding dress; she was already showing signs of skill with the needle, a trade that stood her in good stead in the years that followed. They lived in the house with Lisa's parents, a happy arrangement, and the normal way of the immigrants then. The loss of their father Dimitrio was a bitter blow, when he died in 1922 within a year of their marriage. Her mother was left to bring up three youngsters. Tony was only 12 at the time, and Tilli and Victor were in their teens. The two boys were outstanding athletes and represented the borough of Holborn in the London Schoolboys Athletic Championships.

Lisa had her first son, Renato (Ronnie), in 1924. For three years life was good; Gioacchino was working, Lisa was dressmaking. The family had plenty of friends and Lisa was a very lively, vibrant young woman, quick to learn, and always ready to listen to her neighbours' problems and to help them where possible.

Fate dealt the family a terrible blow when Tony, aged 17, her handsome, outstandingly athletic young brother, began showing signs of a mysterious debilitating illness. After a long period of different diagnoses, the last one was shocking: Parkinson's disease, a progressive, incurable malady, extremely rare in those as young as Tony. It was a nightmare to watch the young lad deteriorate. Lisa, with Gioacchino, was her mother's rock at this terrible time. At first it wasn't too bad, Tony was at least still mobile and they coped.

Victor (see also p 64) went to live in America, where he stayed for 5 years. Tilli married and set up home nearby. Lisa's second son Giuseppe (Pip, or Pippi when little) was born in 1931. Victor came home from his travels in 1933, causing great excitement when his trunks arrived. Ronnie, who was 8 or 9 at the time, remembered the large trunks filling up the hallway. Victor had returned to help his mother financially and to give her some assistance with Tony, whose decreasing mobility would have been too much of a burden for her.

At last, Lisa with her husband Gioacchino and their children were able to move into a home of their own. It was just across the road from her mother, in rooms over the 'Comitti' business premises, where many other Italian families were settled in happy accord. Their little family was complete when Lisa gave birth to her third son, Vittorio (Victor), in 1937. All in all the 1930s was a period of relative contentment for most of the Italians in the quarter. Although it was a time of unrest and a period of unemployment for many, men like Gioacchino, who had a good trade, were able to continue working. He was also a voluntary steward at the well-known Mazzini-Garibaldi Club. Lisa supplemented the family income with her dressmaking. She made the wedding dresses for many of her neighbours and friends. Her sons Ronnie and Pip were doing well at St Peter's Italian school.

The rooms in No.49 were always buzzing with activities of one kind or another, the boys were growing up and their friends were always welcome. The neighbours' children all loved 'Auntie,' as she was known to them. If any of the children tore their clothes, they would go to her and she would mend them, unknown to their mothers, so the children were spared the kind of chastisement that the Mammas were wont to dish out. After all, clothes cost money and some of the families were loth to spend money replacing garments that still had some wear left in them.

In 1939 the outbreak of WW II cast its shadow and the entry of Italy into the war on the side of Germany on 10 June 1940 created panic among the Italian community. Winston Churchill decreed: 'Collar the lot!' and within a few days Gioacchino, whose only connection to any form of 'political' organisation was working at the Mazzini-Garibaldi Club, in essence a working men's club, was picked up by the authorities and sent off to be interned.

This quiet, gentle man, respected and loved, was never seen again. On 2 July the *Arandora Star*, a former cruise ship carrying many Italian as well as German internees in the Irish Sea on their way to Canada, had been torpedoed by a German U-boat. When the news began to seep through the community, no one knew how many Italians were lost, or even whether their husbands or sons were on board. Several days later Lisa was informed that her husband had been on the ship and was now reported missing. The family were stunned. Victor tried

to find out what was going on. He went to the Admiralty where they confirmed
that Gioacchino had been on the ship and that as there had been survivors, he was
still considered to be "missing". Lisa suffered torment, not knowing, hoping and
praying for news. One or two of the men who had been reported missing did turn
up much later on. Ten months of agony went by before the official confirmation
arrived: Gioacchino had perished, along with 450 others.

I met Lisa in 1948 when I was taken to see Ronnie's family by my husband
Bruno, to whom I had recently become engaged. I was struck by the atmosphere in

The Arandora Star at Venice before the war

the home. Her sister Tilli was there with her little daughter Stephanie. Tony, who
by this time was seriously handicapped, was seated at the table. He was living with
Lisa now. He was still very handsome and in spite of his adversity had a saucy look
in his eye and was inclined to flirt. The atmosphere was extremely friendly and I
was made to feel most welcome. Lisa was an excellent conversationalist, she was
an avid listener to the radio and was well informed in the fields of world affairs and
politics. She had firm opinions and, as one of her sons once remarked, "She would
have made a good Prime Minister".

There was contentment in that home and a good deal of laughter. She told
me a story about Pippi, who was a strong lusty child, but he had a secret! When he
was about six years old, he was still demanding a baby's bottle containing broth.
When he fancied his bottle, if there happened to be any visitors in the room he
would start ordering them to go. "Tell her to go" he would shout in no uncertain
terms. The visitor would leave, not knowing why this normally well-behaved little
boy had turned on them. Having dismissed any outsiders he would sit down on
the settee and indulge himself. If you were ever to see Pippi in later life, you will
understand how he came to be such a big, strapping fellow.

Lisa was a remarkable woman. She continued to support her family by
dressmaking, and her children were always impeccably turned out. The boys
helped her with Tony, who had put on a lot of weight because of his immobility.

When the weather was fine they helped Tony down the stairs onto a chair outside the house, where he would contentedly watch the world go by; passers-by all knew him and would stop and chat with him.

In the late 1940s Lisa moved with her sons, her mother (Giuseppina Zanetti) and her brothers Tony and Victor into a house at 93 Little Gray's Inn Lane (now a part of Mount Pleasant). The improvement in lifestyle here was having the luxury of a bathroom. With a family member as severely handicapped as Tony, this must have felt like heaven on earth. Lisa was still full of boundless energy, dressmaking, keeping the family on an even keel, cooking and tending to Tony's needs, which became more demanding as his Parkinson's disease progressed. Brother Victor helped to finance not only his ageing mother but the vast amount of expense that accrued due to Tony's illness. The family never gave up on Tony. Hospitals, doctors and medication bills were endless; specialists were consulted, but to no avail.

Lisa's mother Giuseppina died in 1949. Ronnie and Pippi were working, Ronnie as an apprentice jeweller in Hatton Garden, Pip, following so many other lads from the Quarter, in the terrazzo trade. The youngest son, young Victor, was still attending St Peter's Italian School.

When the family made their final move, it was to a new block of flats in a turning off Theobald's Road, about a 10-minute walk from the Italian Quarter. In comparison to their earlier home, this was luxury indeed: there were lifts up to the three-bedroom flat and everything was on one level with a beautifully equipped kitchen, and it was close to buses and shops.

At this time all Lisa's sons were in full employment and she continued with her dressmaking. Here, as in their previous homes, there was a constant stream of visitors. Lisa had time for everyone and she was popular with her new neighbours. If the children who lived in the flats arrived home from school to find their mothers were out, they would go straight to Auntie's (as Lisa was known), where they would be made welcome with a drink or a biscuit, and chat happily to Lisa and Tony until their parent returned.

When her sons married, Lisa made beautiful wedding dresses for each of her daughters-in-law. She was now coping with Tony alone, although her sons were always at hand to help when he needed to be taken to the doctor or the hospital. To the family's dismay Lisa's sight began to fail and it was discovered that she had a ruptured retina. An operation improved things for a time but her eyesight was impaired, and this hampered her a great deal in her later years.

When Lisa could no longer cope with Tony's care, the family reluctantly let him go into a nursing home in Camden. Lisa and Tilli visited him daily without fail, and in the evenings her sons and Tony's friends would go to see him. Every weekend, when extra help was available, he would be brought home to Lisa's flat, where he would join the family dinner and afterwards play the inevitable card games.

The kind of love and care Lisa lavished on her young brother until his death in 1981 at the age of 73 tells us the kind of woman she was – one of life's angels.

Menozzi–Zanetti family

Victor Zanetti, the ballroom champion

Victor, the older of Lisa's two brothers, played a large part in her life. He had great presence, charisma and a sense of purpose, which became apparent in his youth. In the 1920s he was employed as a steward on an ocean liner and when it docked in New York, he jumped ship with two other lads. His fellows were soon apprehended and deported, but he was not. Victor got a job at the famous Waldorf Hotel in New York, where in a very short time he was promoted to the post of restaurant manager.

Victor Barrat and Doreen Freeman, World Ballroom Dancing Champions

He returned to England in 1933; during his time in America he developed his avid interest in ballroom dancing. During WW II, while working as head waiter at the Café de Paris, a West End night club, he spent all his leisure time studying and practising what at that time was just a hobby. He left the Café de Paris to allow more time to pursue his dream of becoming a professional ballroom dancer. Six months later the night club was bombed when it was full of patrons, servicemen and their girls. Nephew Ronnie remembered his uncle's anguish when he returned from the scene, where he had gone to seek news of friends and colleagues. The list of dead and injured was immense.

Victor was now entering serious dancing contests and winning everything. He started to teach, in the early days just a small class, held in one of the rooms at the Mazzini-Garibaldi Club in Red Lion Street. As his career progressed, Victor, in view of the attitude to foreigners in the 1940s, changed his professional name to Victor Barrat. The next step was the Victor Barrat School of Dancing in Regent Street.

In the competitive world of ballroom dancing the name Victor Barrat became associated with the best. In 1948/49, with wife Doreen Freeman as partner, they won the world ballroom championships. Victor's continuing success was assured. Ballroom dancing at that time was at the height of its popularity. He opened another flourishing school in Knightsbridge. Victor was not only a wonderful performer, he was a born teacher. He taught the art of ballroom dancing to many famous people and was in great demand. He choreographed the dancing sequences in the successful English film *Spring in Park Lane* and coached the stars of the film, Anna Neagle and Michael Wilding. Later he went to America, where he coached Marilyn Monroe and Victor Mature.

The Menozzi family followed Victor's career with pride. Lisa's experience with the needle also came into play, in the making of many of Victor's partner's ballroom gowns.

Coffee bars began to spring up in the West End in the 1960s. 'The Macabre', one of the earliest, was situated in Soho in a little alleyway between Wardour Street and Dean Street. It is remembered by many on account of its eerie décor: the walls were black, the tables were in the shape of coffins and the ashtrays were skeleton heads. Dismembered bodies and cobwebs hung from the ceilings and in the nooks and crannies. Strange! but the customers loved it, and it became famous as one of the places to see whilst visiting Soho. Ronnie was the manager, assisted by his fiancée, Joe, who later became his wife.

Lisa outlived both of her brothers: Victor died prematurely in 1970 at the age of 62. Sadly, Lisa's failing eyesight blighted the end of her days. She lived on in poor health after Tony's death in 1981. Lisa died in 1985, aged 81, sorely missed by her family and the many friends she had made throughout her life, which began in the Italian Quarter in 1904.

Tricoli family

The Tricoli brothers, plus Harry Doncaster (who supplied the photograph)

A well-known family "down the Hill" were Mr & Mrs Tricoli, who lived in Summer Street and moved several times around The Hill to different addresses.

This was a 'mixed' marriage, Mr Tricoli was Greek and his wife was Italian. They had five sons who were popular down the Hill, their sense of humour being second to none.

Their English was excellent but in a conversation with Manoli regarding his daughter's wedding, he described his apparel on the day, saying he had got 'a luvely whistle' and a 'smart trilby'. His pièce de résistance on all occasions was his rendering of '*That's Amore*'.

All the boys were extremely smart.

Servini and Giacon families

In 1860 in the tiny mountain village of Villora (Parma) Domenico Servini's wife, Rosa Servini, née Copelotti, gave birth to twins – a boy, Pietro, and a girl, Elisabetta. Domenico was the proprietor of Villora's only *osteria*. In the years that followed the family increased to seven children – another girl and four boys. We are going to follow the life of the first-born son, Pietro. Pietro Servini grew up in the village and eventually married Giovanna Marzolini. The couple lived in the *osteria* with his parents. It was a fruitful marriage: Giovanna gave birth to sixteen children, but lost six in childbirth.

With too little room in the house, nine little mouths to feed and finances being stretched to their limit, it made sense for the sons to go out into the world and seek a better livelihood. In 1901 Pietro's son, 16-year-old Domenico Servini, travelled to England accompanied by one of his uncles. Arriving in London they made their way to Eyre Street Hill, to an address where an earlier immigrant from Villora had a lodging house.

Domenico soon found work with one of the asphalt companies, a trade which accommodated many other Italian immigrants He was very young and suffered badly from homesickness. He shed many a tear into his pillow; he missed not only his family and friends but his beloved horse. Asphalting was not for him, but he soon found another job, as a kitchen hand in the Savoy Hotel, a job which suited him and where he soon progressed to assisting the chefs by preparing the vegetables and making the sauces. He sent every penny of his wages home to his parents.

News from home wasn't good. His uncle Giovanni had journeyed with an expedition to Alaska in search of gold. The group did indeed discover a gold mine but their success was short-lived. The Russian authorities confiscated the mine, leaving the party destitute. When his uncle returned to Villora he was suffering from frostbite and his health had deteriorated. A family conference decided that, as there was no question of Giovanni leaving the village, he should take over the *osteria* with his family and Pietro, their father, should join his son Domenico in England. He made the journey alone, leaving his wife, Giovanna, and the children in the village.

Domenico's circumstances had improved. He was now living in improved accommodation in Mount Pleasant and he was overjoyed to see his father again. Pietro soon found a job and subsequently sent for his wife and children. The family settled down in their new home, the children attended St Peter's Italian School and soon there was a new arrival, a baby son, Giuseppe (Pip).

By 1910 finances were looking up, both men had jobs, in fact things were so improved that arrangements were made for Pietro's mother, Rosa, to make the journey from Villora to visit her son and grandson. During her stay with them, a young girl, Maria Bazzini, whose family lived in a village near Villora, came to the house to see Rosa and hear if she had news of her family at home. Destiny stepped in and Domenico Servini, who had come home from work early suffering from a bad toothache, arrived in time to see the young visitor. He took one look at the pretty young girl and was hit by the thunderbolt! As he was heard to remark later "When I

Pietro, Domenico and Tonino Servini outside the shop in Mount Pleasant

first set eyes on Maria she looked like "*una pesca appena matura*" (a freshly ripened peach). A year later, in 1911, the happy couple were married at St Peter's Italian Church; their honeymoon was a day spent in the green fields of Hampstead Heath.

Naturally, they started married life living with the rest of the family in the rooms over their shop in Mount Pleasant.

In 1921 they found the means to start out on their own, the name *D Servini* went up over a second shop and the family were in business. It was one of the first delicatessen shops in London owned by Italians. Life went well for the families. Business was good and in the same year Maria gave birth to a baby boy, Italo.

Domenico was overjoyed, but he didn't have much time to enjoy his baby boy because in 1914 he was called up to serve in the Italian Army. Since he was now proficient in English he acted as interpreter for the British troops fighting in Italy.

The business suffered; his father Pietro kept the shop open, but supplies from Europe were limited and, of course, they were extremely worried about others in the family. Back in Villora some of their cousins were also serving in the Italian Army.

In 1918, at the war's end, Domenico returned home, the business recovered and life returned to normal. Two years later their daughter, Marinetta, was born. But six weeks later his mother Giovanna died. Maria, still recovering from the recent birth, was relieved when her good friend and neighbour Mary Zanelli offered

Domenico Servini (far right) with Maria holding Italo outside the second shop

to mind baby Marinetta during the funeral. Mary Zanelli had recently herself given birth to a baby son Ettore (Ecci). On the morning of the funeral, Maria took the precious baby girl into her home and placed her in the cot with baby Ecci.

When Maria returned heavy-hearted from the funeral, she went to the Zanelli home and collected her baby, took her home, fed her and put her in her cot, where she slept peacefully for a time. Subsequently, when she cried, Maria picked her up in order to change her nappy, unwound the swaddling bands in which it was the custom to wrap infants in those days, and discovered that she had brought home the wrong baby! It was a boy! In spite of the sadness of the occasion, the incident made everyone smile.

Marinetta recalls her childhood as the happiest of times; she was thoroughly spoilt by her *Nonno* (Grandfather) Pietro and by her young uncles and aunts. In 1923 her brother Italo delighted the family by winning a scholarship to St Ignatius Grammar School. He was one of the first boys from St Peter's Italian School to win this scholarship. When Marinetta was five a baby sister, Giovanna Servini, completed Dominic's family. In those days when a baby was born, relatives or neighbours rallied round: one would do the shopping, another take care of the other children and keep the home going, and see that the new father had a meal ready and waiting at the end of his working day. The men had to continue working, as jobs were hard to come by and paternity leave was unheard of. Of course there were hardships, but the feeling of belonging to a community greatly enriched the lives of these early immigrant families.

As Pietro's business prospered, Domenico decided that it was time to leave Mount Pleasant and set up elsewhere. Many a tear was shed for the old times when, in 1929, he moved with Maria and the children into rooms above his new

Servini delicatessen in Killick Street, King's Cross, about half an hour's walk from Mount Pleasant. It turned out to be a wise move. Many of their old customers and friends had moved into the area and they welcomed the new deli; they came regularly on Saturdays for their Italian produce and a chat about the old days.

Life in the Italian Quarter was changing. In the 1930s many of the families were being rehoused in the outer areas of the inner city, whilst others, who had accumulated money through their labours, were moving further afield, to Highbury, Highgate, Barnsbury or the Angel, none of which was far away from their old homes in the quarter; the families and their offspring still attended St Peter's Church and the Italian School.

Marinetta and her younger sister Giovanna continued their education at St Peter's Italian School. Domenico, who had a great love of music and a passion for opera, Verdi in particular, possessed a fine tenor voice. In his time he had heard Caruso, Gigli and Tito Schipa sing. Music filled the home and where there is music, you will generally find happiness. He passed his passion for music on to his children. The young Giovanna was showing great potential as a soprano.

Following in her brother Italo's footsteps, at the age of 11 Marinetta won a scholarship to St Aloysius Girls' Convent in Euston and was followed five years later by her sister Giovanna. Marinetta matriculated when she was 17. Maths was her forte and she badly wanted to go to university to continue her studies, but her mother advised her to learn a trade first. It was agreed that she should learn dressmaking and go to university at a later date. The decision was a disappointment at the time but Marinetta said: "I have never regretted it, as my dressmaking skills have stood me in good stead for many years".

By 1939 war clouds were gathering and, when the inevitable happened, Domenico's youngest brother Guiseppe (Pip), who had long since left Clerkenwell, was living in Liverpool, where he had been sent on a job for the terrazzo company he worked for. He was married to an English girl, Rose, and they had four little ones. He was called up into the British Army and like so many other young men at that time, he had to leave his wife and young children. Little did they dream as they said their goodbyes that five years would elapse before they set eyes on him again. He was sent to Burma and did not return until 1946 after the war ended.

Italo, Marinetta's older brother, was more fortunate than his uncle; he was also called up into the British Army, but he remained in England where he eventually became an interpreter in the Italian prisoner-of-war camps. During his time in the army he met and married an English girl, Mary Brickly. When he was home on leave he told his parents, Domenico and Maria, about the unhappy state of some of the Italian POWs: homesick youngsters, married men missing their wives and children, others frantic because they had lost contact with their families and had no knowledge of their fate. Many of them had come from areas that had been rent asunder by the fighting in their homeland. Domenico and Maria began to visit the camps on Sundays and bring what consolation they could to the men. They would take them some of Maria's home cooking, listen to their problems and help them trace news of relatives back in Italy. Domenico worked tirelessly for the welfare of the prisoners and was later made a *Cavaliere* by the Italian government for his work.

Enter Bepi Giacon

One Sunday they took Marinetta with them to the camp at South Mimms. Here she first set eyes on one of the prisoners, Guiseppe (Bepi) Giacon. That meeting changed Marinetta's life. The couple began chatting and she learnt that he was a *Granatiere* (Grenadier) *di Savoia*. After that first meeting she returned with her parents to South Mimms as often as she could to visit him. In the months that followed, she learnt that Bepi had served in the Italian army for 9 years and he was one of nine children. He hadn't seen his family, who lived in Padua,

Wedding of Marinetta Servini and Bepi (Giuseppe) Giacon (November 1947) after 5 years of separation. Bridesmaids cousins Rene Servini, Mary Bazzini, Maria Inzani; sister Giovanna Servini to her left.

all that time. Just as their relationship was blossoming into something deeper, Bepi was moved to another camp in Norwich. Undaunted, they corresponded daily; they were separated for 3 years and in that period she visited him on only five occasions, each time chaperoned by a married cousin or her sister-in-law. When the war ended Bepi was repatriated. Nothing changed except that her letters were now being sent to Italy.

Before being taken prisoner Bepi had been involved in serious action and he was later awarded a silver medal for bravery. Eighteen months elapsed before Bepi again set foot in England, but on 16 November 1947 they tied the knot that bound them together for more than fifty years.

They made their first home with Marinetta's parents above the deli in Killick Street, as their forebears had done. Bepi assisted his father-in-law Domenico in the business. Their first baby, a daughter, Anna, was born in 1948 and Anna was followed in fairly quick succession by eight siblings!

In 1956 women drivers were becoming a familiar sight, so Marinetta decided that it was time she joined the world of the modern woman. She began to take driving lessons, but she hadn't got far into the course when she found that she was pregnant. "Oh well, there's always another day," but there wasn't. Marinetta made another two attempts at driving lessons but each time she was thwarted.

Over the years Bepi continued to help his father-in-law, Domenico, to run the business. In the little house they had subsequently bought Marinetta not only raised her large family but also made all their clothes, and, in addition, wedding dresses for friends and relatives. St Peter's Italian Church bazaar benefited greatly from her prowess with the needle – cushions and aprons were churned out by the

Beniamino Gigli singing in the Mass at St Peter's Italian church

dozen. Bepi too was far from idle. Aside from the long hours in the deli, in 1965 he was responsible for reviving Italian classes for second- and third-generation Italian children, where they could learn Italian grammar and the history of their antecedents. (In the 1960s Italian language was not included on the average school curriculum.) The first classes were held in Copenhagen Street, Islington. Since then they have spread to many other suburban areas and towns, wherever there are communities of Italian families. Bepi remained deeply involved in this projext and worked on many other committees involving Italian culture and community work, until his death in 2004. Over 1,000 people crammed themselves into the Italian Church for his funeral service.

Domenico and his wife Maria moved to Highgate, where they lived next door to Marinetta's young sister, Giovanna, who was married to Ivo Cardetti, a dedicated and active member of the Mazzini-Garibaldi Club and of the Italian Church choir. Giovanna too had a magnificent soprano voice. For many years she sang in the church choir and was the soloist at all weddings and funerals. She was there when the world's greatest tenor, Beniamino Gigli, visited the church and sang with the choir. She also spent many happy hours with her parents listening to operas, particularly those of Verdi. Music was the great love of her life.

Grandfather Domenico died in 1975, aged 90. The young boy who had left the little village of Villora in 1902 was at peace, he had achieved his aim: he had made a good life here in England with hard work and dedication to his family, his business and his work in the community. Maria, his wife, died in 1981 at the age of 89.

The deli on the corner of Killick Street (p 70) continued to be a weekly shopping stop for many of the old Italians from The Hill. The little house along the road in Southern Street was always filled with the chatter, laughter and music of the young Giacons and their friends.

The youngsters began to move out, some to marry, others seeking the independence that young people of today's generation insist on. One thing remains unchanged, that is the family gathering in the house in Southern Street every Friday evening for one of *Mamma's* Italian dinners, for amongst Marinetta's many talents her culinary expertise is second to none, exemplified by her famous recipes printed in the Backhill magazine for many years, and closely followed by many young readers.

The Giacon family can still be found at the Procession and *Sagra* each year, fulfilling many of the tasks that go to make that very special day the success that it is.

Seven Nastri brothers

Recounted to Olive Besagni by the seventh son, Victor

RICCIARDELLI GIOVANNI
LAMBERTI LUCIA

Giovanni Ricciardelli and his wife (née Lamberti)

In 1891, in the little fishing village of Minori (Salerno), Southern Italy, Trofimena Ricciardelli was born. She was one of five children, three girls and two boys. Her father Giovanni was a farmer, and as with so many of the families in the area, life was hard: too many mouths to feed and too few resources. The Ricciardellis' first attempt at relocation was to Brazil. Things didn't work out, and they returned to Minori, where her parents spent the rest of their days. Two of the elder girls later emigrated to South America.

In 1908, when Trofimena was seventeen, she was being courted by a young lad from Ravello, Alfonso Nastri. Her parents wished to put an end to the relationship, so it was agreed that she should join her older sisters in South America, but then the plan was changed and arrangements were made to send her to a cousin who had settled in England.

When the ship docked at Southampton the bewildered young girl was in a state of shock when her cousin turned up and claimed her. She was taken to a house in Battersea, South London, 15A Falcon Road, where she was put to work as a domestic.

Back in Ravello, a picturesque village on a small mountain overlooking Minori, the young Alfonso was pining for his sweetheart. He came from a smaller family than most: he had only one brother, Andrea and one sister, Maddalena. Their father Nicole, usually shortened to Nicol', was the local barber, whose customers would sit outside the basilica while he performed his artistry with scissors and razor in the open air, in full view of the passers-by.

In the words of Trofimena, repeated quite often over the years to her sons: "I wasn't that keen, but he wanted to marry me so he followed me". Being young and Italian, he took matters into his own hands. He had the means because he had worked from the age of 12 in local cafés and trattorias, and now, at the age of seventeen, he was proficient in culinary matters, particularly in the preparation and cooking of fish. He had a trade, he had the fare, so it wasn't too long before he was on his way to England and his love.

Alfonso's first address was in Little Pultney Street, Soho, above the premises where he worked. He traced Trofimena to Battersea and the courtship began. It was no mean trek in those days, the only affordable means of transport being the horse-drawn tram. The courtship lasted seven years; it couldn't have been easy, as they both worked long and unsocial hours, and there is no doubt that part of their earnings were sent home, to help the parents back in Salerno. The outbreak of WW I interfered with the forthcoming nuptials, but finally the wedding took place in the Church of the Sacred Heart on 25 November 1915.

Once wed, the couple headed for Clerkenwell. Their first home was in Myddelton Street, a short distance from The Hill. Within the year their first-born, a son, Alfonso (Fonso) junior had arrived. Shortly after the baby's birth Alfonso received his call-up papers; he was to return to Italy and join the

Seven Nastri brothers

Alfonso Nastri in Italian Army uniform

Italian Army. They packed their bags and set off on the long journey back to Salerno, where Alfonso left Trofimena (who was expecting a second baby) and little Fonso in the care of the Ricciardelli family, and went off to join his unit. Much to his wife and family's relief he was put into the catering corps, where he served as a cook for the duration of the war. During this time they were blessed with a second son, baby Nicol', the only one of their children to be born in Italy.

In 1918, the war over, the little family returned to Clerkenwell, where they rented rooms at No.23 Great Bath Street, in the heart of Little Italy, over the Fratellanza Club. The accommodation consisted of two rooms, a shared outside sink and a communal outside toilet; the rent was six shillings and sixpence a week. Alfonso soon found a job as a chef in the West End. Trofimena was happy in her new home. At least she was amongst her own kind. Even though the dialects were many and varied, the majority were Italians, which helped her overcome her periodic homesickness. It wasn't too long before the inevitable happened and another boy, Antonio Nastri, was born.

1922 was a bad year for the young couple: the baby, Antonio (Tony) suffered from fits, and died at the age of 11 months. During this same period, Fonso, who was 6, was in hospital. He had been kicked in the hip by a horse while playing in Warner Street, sustaining an injury which plagued him for the rest of his life. Later, when the funeral was over and Fonso was brought home from the hospital, his mother was shocked when he said "I know baby Tony isn't here because he came and said goodbye to me in the hospital." Trofimena didn't know what to think, but even today the story is repeated throughout the family.

The undertaker's invoice for the baby's funeral was as follows: Baby's white satin lined coffin, plus carriages and black horses with plumes, five pounds, plus three shillings for memorial cards. When you think that that amount was equal to 15 weeks' rent, what a financial punch on the nose that must have been. But they survived.

Giovanni Nastri (Shorty), son number four, made his appearance in 1923, followed by Pasqua in 1925, then Guiseppe (Joe Joe) in 1927. By this time Trofimena was wondering if she was ever going to be blessed with a daughter, for as much as she loved her sons, she was often heard to say "if I only had just one girl". The years spent over the club in Bath Street were hard years for the parents. It is difficult to imagine how they coped with the washing alone: the clothes, no disposable nappies, plus the cooking, the mending, the cleaning and the shopping. On the whole the boys have good memories of their childhood years in the quarter. *Papa* Nastri was rarely out of work. He was employed as a chef in some of London's prestigious hotels like the Savoy and at Simpson's, but the hours were long and taxing. Often he would set off at 8 am and not return until 1 am the following morning. In comparison to the breadwinners in some of the other families, the money was good, and as perks of the job he was able to supplement the family larder with titbits brought home from work. But with six hungry boys needing to be fed, clothed and shod money was tight. There were compensations: plenty of friends were living in the same circumstances, although, as Pasqua remarked, "We had our own friends, but, as we were all near enough of an age, we brothers always had one another".

At least Trofimena was able to communicate with the other *mammas*, some of whom came from the same area in southern Italy. She rarely complained about the noise of the boys playing, and the new babies soon got used to the sound of their brothers' indoor games and pellet fights going on around them. Their mother was never idle; if she wasn't washing, ironing, cooking or cleaning, she was sewing. Nevertheless, she was always singing, mostly Neapolitan songs, 'Santa Lucia' and 'Funiculi Funicula' being her favourites.

1931 found them at a new address in Warner Street. One of the reasons for the move was to achieve the luxury of having their own sink, albeit on the stairs; at least it wasn't communal, which must have seemed like heaven. It was here that son number seven, Victor, was born – seven in a row! Even in The Quarter that must have been a record.

After four years, another move, this time to Victoria Dwellings in Clerkenwell Road. Here they had their own front door, but the flat was above another family who probably complained about the noise, and who could blame them! This prompted another move, in 1935, this time to a basement flat in Cavendish

Mansions. What a sigh of relief Trofimena must have given, when she no longer had to worry about the noise of the boys over other people's heads. By the time the family moved to Cavendish Mansions, some of the financial pressure had eased. Fonso and Nicol' were working and, like the majority of the lads from The Quarter, started off in the catering trade as commis waiters, though later on they found employment in statuette factories. Eventually, in 1946, two of the boys settled for floor laying and eventually formed their own floor-laying company.

Giovanni (Shorty) had different ideas of a career. As a youngster he acted as runner for the local street-corner bookies and eventually he became a tic-tac man on race courses.

Pasqua Nastri, a very congenial character, began his working life as a page boy at a grand hotel but could not settle, so he tried his luck in the statuette trade, where he could enjoy the company of his friends. The latter period of his working life he spent working in the printing trade.

Papa was still working exceedingly long hours and Victor recalled his father alighting from the bus at the top of Clerkenwell Road, where he would remove his shoes and walk the rest of the way in his stockinged feet. Pasqua, son number five, remembered that his dad always rubbed spirits into the soles of his feet, to harden them against the many hours that he spent standing in the heat of the kitchens. Victor was heard to remark "My father was smaller than me, but in my eyes he was 10 feet tall, and as for my older brothers, I looked upon them as my heroes. I was always really proud of them".

Trofimena did most of her shopping in Leather Lane, where there was a shop, referred to by many of the Italian *mammas* at the time as '*Paun Broc*' (Pawn Broker). This was in fact a shop divided into two sections: one side was a pawnbroker, where poor families would take their husband's Sunday suits in on a Monday and retrieve them on a Friday; even bed linen was pawned as a last resort to obtain a little cash. The other section of the shop was Harvey and Thompson who sold run-of-the-mill bed linens and cheap clothes that were sold in similar shops everywhere. Most of the children living in the quarter at the time remember being taken to Harvey and Thompson for their outfits.

It must have been a shock for Trofimena when, at the age of 45, she found that she was pregnant once more. Surely, she must have thought, this one has to be the longed-for daughter. But it wasn't: along came Carlo. The last chance for a daughter had slipped away. Eight boys in a row!

Like their parents all the boys were shorter than average, which never worried them for a moment. A typical sense of humour prevailed amongst the Italian boys and girls at the time and constant good-natured teasing went on. Pasqua laughingly said, without a trace of resentment, "They used to call us The Seven Dwarfs".

When asked what they remembered about Christmas as children, the boys answered in unison, "Wonderful! our Christmases were wonderful". "Did you get lots of presents?" "Oh no, well, maybe sometimes a little box of chocolates or something like that. At Christmas my Dad would cook the dinner, as incidentally he did every Sunday, and as he was a good chef, you can imagine the kind of meal was put in front of us for Christmas Dinner." Pasqua, who is a little on the chubby side, added, "No one could cook squid like our Dad". He was positively salivating as he spoke, and as we have seen earlier, the cooking of fish and seafood was Alfonso's speciality. " You see," Victor continued, "When my Dad used to sit at the head of the table, he would look with such pride on his little wife and his seven sons, some of them now grown into young men. You could see he was a happy, proud man."

Joe Joe, like his brothers, left school at 14 for a job as doorman at The Ivy, an exclusive restaurant used by some of the most famous glitterati, film stars and politicians; anyone who was anyone would be seen dining there. He was promoted to the job of wine waiter, but like his brothers before him, he didn't remain in the catering trade and eventually found work in printing, a much sought-after job.

Victor followed in the same pattern as his brothers. He started at The Ivy as a commis waiter, but later went into floor laying, where he remained for 40 years.

Carlo, a talented footballer, became a football coach; he spent two years in Australia where he managed a football team. He returned to England and is now working as a PE instructor in London schools.

Each of the boys attended St Peter's Italian School. Between 1919 and 1952 there was always a Nastri as a pupil there. They took part in sporting activities, each one playing for the school team in their respective years. When asked if they ever felt threatened outside the confines of The Quarter on account of their obvious Italian-ness, Pasqua said that he did to a degree, but that it was worse during the war years. Victor volunteered "Whenever we represented the school in competitive athletics or football, we always felt that we were competing for Italy, rather than the school."

In 1955 Alfonso and Trofimena thought of going to Salerno for a holiday and to visit their respective families. They felt that the boys were now grown, Carlo was 18 and it was time to enjoy the fruits of their labours. But *Papa* Alfonso Nastri died quite suddenly in March. Trofimena did eventually return to her old home, when she recovered from her loss, but it was with Carlo. She visited the village where Nicol' was born and, naturally, her parents' home. When she returned she said that, although she had enjoyed seeing everyone in the old country she was glad to return to England and her sons. Ma, as the boys called her, always told her sons, " This is the country that has given you an education and the opportunity to make a living and you must abide by its laws". She loved England and clearly considered herself to be Anglo-Italian.

The Nastri sons (with the exception of Johnny (Shorty), who remained with his mother until she died at 88) all married English girls, all had good marriages. Trofimena lived long enough to attend all her sons' weddings and there are many Nastris growing up in England today as a result of that journey made by Trofimena and Alfonso way back in the year 1908.

It was a shock for the family when Nicol' suffered a fatal stroke at the early age of 59. 1982 brought more sorrow when Giuseppe (Joe Joe) died of a heart attack, leaving his wife Pat and 6-year-old daughter Natalie. Two years later they lost Giovanni (Shorty). Victor said "Wonderful as it is to be part of a large family, you get a greater amount of grief as you lose them one by one, particularly if you are one of the youngest."

Nicol' (Nicole) Nastri, War Hero

Nicol' was the only one of the Nastri boys born in Italy, because his parents returned to Salerno before he was born, when his father Alfonso was called up into the Italian Army.

Nicol' Nastri in British Army uniform

On 2 September 1939, at the beginning of the *second* World War, Nicol' was in the first contingent of young men called up to serve in the British Army .

As with most of the young conscripts, despite having to leave his beloved parents and brothers, he soon settled down to the training. Naturally, like all serving Anglo-Italians, he was hoping that Italy, if it came into the war, would come in on the side of Britain and France. Alas, on 10 June 1940, to the consternation of all the Italian communities in Britain, Italy entered on the side of Germany.

Nicol' received a letter from home telling him that there was a "very real threat" that his father, Alfonso, was about to be interned. He was appalled, and requested an interview with his commanding officer. He asked if anything could be done to save his father from being interned.

The next day, the CO told him that if he would be prepared to volunteer for a Special Service Unit they would see what they could do with regard to keeping his father out of an internment camp. He volunteered without hesitation.

Back in Clerkenwell, in the Nastri home, tearful preparations were being made for *Papa's* imminent arrest. Then the authorities came and told Alfonso that he was to register as an alien, to report to the local police station once a week and not to go outside a 5-mile radius of the Italian Quarter. They also removed the family's wireless. You can imagine the family's rejoicing. They had no idea that Alfonso had been saved by Nicol's sacrifice.

Nine months later, Private Nastri arrived home on 4 days' leave. Victor recalled that he was wearing a very impressive full kit. However, Nicol' said nothing about his special assignment. He simply told them when he left that he would write to them as usual. Pasqua remembers going to King's Cross Station with his brother John (Shorty) to see him off. They said their farewells; "Look after Mum" was the last thing he said as he embraced them. It would be 5 years before they set eyes on him again.

The 'Special Service Unit' was in fact the beginnings of the S.A.S. The first inkling the volunteers had of what was to follow was when they were sent to the Central Landing School, where they were informed that they were now 'X' troop, No.2 Commando and were to be trained as parachutists. They were instructed never to talk about their training or activities and that it was all "top secret". The training was rigorous and the squad were encouraged to believe that they were unique, the fittest men in the army. Following their ground training they began to jump from aircraft, "It's as easy as falling out of bed," they were told. "All you have to do is jump."

One of the men was killed when his parachute failed to open. The training jumps stopped for a while, whilst new methods of folding the 'chutes were tested. After a brief respite, the jumping recommenced. There were no further casualties.

The next move was to Fort William in Scotland, to join 'The School of Irregular Warfare'. Here further training took the form of mountain climbing, swimming while carrying full kit, and the use of weapons of war etc. Until then the word *paratrooper* was unheard-of. It was there that Trooper Nastri found himself early in 1941, after 9 months of training, one of 36 specially selected volunteers who were about to take part in Operation Colossus.

'X' Troop was flown to Malta in Whitley aircraft, and then dropped 60 miles inland from the coast of Southern Italy. Their objective was to blow up an enormous aqueduct in the region of Campagna, about 30 miles from Salerno. The aqueduct spanned a gorge over the Tragino River, in the heart of difficult, mountainous terrain; it was the main water supply for Apulia and several other provinces where there were dockyards and armaments factories.

In the final stages of the training the troop were joined by an Italian civilian, Fortunato Picchi. He was a British citizen and an anti-fascist. He and Trooper Nastri were to be the interpreters. For their own safety their names had to be changed: Nicol' was to become Trooper John Tristan (a near anagram of Nastri). Picchi's name was changed to Trooper Pierre Dupont and he was told that in the event of capture he should say that he was of French extraction, because he had a strong non-British accent.

Major Pritchard, head of the command, instructed Nicol' "Stick to me like a limpet. No matter who else gets cut off from me, once we land, you are my ears and my only means of communication."

On 3 February 1941 'X' Troop flew to Malta, where they were kitted out with special clothing in which Italian currency had been sewn into the linings of the tunics and silk maps into the sleeves. Each man was given a metal collar stud and told not to lose it, because there was a tiny compass inserted in the back which would be revealed when the white paint was scratched off. They were issued with special rations, enough to last them for 6 days.

In the early hours of the morning of 10 February, the Whitleys set off on their mission. The terrain surrounding the aqueduct was desolate, mountainous and dangerous, far worse than the officers had been led to expect. The quiet, still, moonlit night made the descent almost magical. The 'chutes floated silently and gracefully down. Nicol' landed on the bank of the river and quickly found Major Pritchard. The Major was relieved to see Nicol', whom he had dubbed his 'Cockney Italian Sparrow'. They silently made their way to the objective. When they arrived at the scene, they found some of the others already there. The first arrivals had found the aqueduct unguarded, with the exception of one Italian soldier whom they had taken prisoner. Several peasants who had left their farms to see what was going on were persuaded to assist them in collecting the 'chutes and other containers that had been dropped. They helped willingly as this was an adventure for them and they welcomed anything to relieve the burden of their daily farming routine.

At this point the Major discovered that the chief engineer had not made it to the meeting-place (they found later that he had dropped into the wrong valley). The job fell to a junior officer, the engineer's assistant, who agreed to do the best he could. He was surprised at the size and the strength of the aqueduct, but he carried on, and did an excellent job. After the explosion, the main piers collapsed and the water cascaded down into the valley. Further along they even managed to blow up a small bridge, which would have been useful to the Germans.

No Italian suffered any harm from the operation. On the whole it was an event which the locals were to enjoy recounting for many years to come. Years after the war Victor, Nicol's younger brother, went to Southern Italy to visit the scene. He found an old farmer who remembered the night clearly, having been a child at the time. He recounted his version of the events that happened that night. "It was such a bright moonlit night and suddenly these frothy, graceful apparitions came floating down through the stars. I called my mother, and some of the other children. They came running out, as did the other farmers in the area. We all gazed up at the sky, not understanding it at all. Then someone said that they were angels floating down from heaven. Some fell to their knees, making the sign of the cross. It was a sight that I have never forgotten," he said.

With the mission accomplished, the only casualty was a Corporal Boulter who had fractured his ankle on landing. The group knew that they had to leave him behind, because the journey on which they were about to embark was too long and dangerous to allow for passengers. Nicol' was aware, as were most of the group, that their chances of making the 60-mile journey to the proposed rendezvous on the coast, where a submarine should be waiting on the 15th and 16th, were slim. They had 5 days in which to get there, and first they had to get out of the Tragino Valley.

It was trial and error all the way, always climbing, an avalanche of slime and mud at one point seriously hampering the ascent. Two days and nights they climbed, only stopping for nourishment and a little rest. They decided to risk marching along the road, in order to make up for the time lost. They formed a column, with Nicol' marching alongside calling out: "No qui, No qui," (Left, Left, in dialect). If they were stopped, Nicol' was to say that they were Austrian troops on secret manoeuvres, troops on a secret mission. Although this entailed more risk of exposure, too much time had already been lost using the more secluded tracks. The original plan was to travel at night, but speed being of the essence, they set off at dusk. It wasn't long before a man riding a bike approached and looked searchingly at them as he rode past. "Buona sera," he said. Nicol' replied, "Buona sera." "Well done," said Major Pritchard. After short distance, the man turned and cycled back. "It's up to you, Trooper, now do your stuff" said Major Pritchard.

"Where are you going?" said the civilian. "I can't tell you," answered Nicol', "we are on a highly secret mission." The man eyed the group. "Who are they? They are not wearing Italian uniforms." Nicol' replied, "they are a mixture of Austrian and Italian troops on manoeuvres. I am the interpreter and, as I said before, this is a highly secret mission. It would be best if you didn't tell anyone you have seen us." The man nodded. He looked nervous. "I understand, I will say nothing." He got back on his bike and rode off into the dusk. Something about the Italian's manner led Nicol' to believe that he hadn't been taken in at all. He said to Major Pritchard, " I'm pretty certain that he's on to us." How right he was. They marched on, but within the hour they were surrounded by Carabinieri from the nearby town of St Andrea, accompanied by vicious-looking dogs.

The sergeant shouted an order. Nicol' translated: "He says we are to throw down our arms, Major." "O.K. men, drop your guns," the Major ordered. The Sergeant pointed his pistol at the Major's head, shouting as did so. "What's the blighter saying, Tristan (Nicol')?" "He wants you to hand over your pistol, Sir." The Major did so. Then the troop were marched down to St Andrea, surrounded by an ever-increasing crowd of locals, who had all turned out to witness this exciting event. On arrival they were met by local dignitaries, and after a short while the military arrived. The Italian officer in charge questioned them in English. He was clearly baffled by their presence, but he had spotted Nicolo's resemblance to the locals. He addressed Major Pritchard, "Can you explain to me what this man is doing here? He is an Italian, he speaks Italian." The Major quickly assured him, "He may look Italian and he does speak Italian, but he is a British soldier." The officer wasn't convinced. Major Pritchard added, "You are an Italian, but as far as I'm concerned, you look English and you can speak English. That doesn't make you an Englishman, does it?" He hoped that he'd convinced him, but looking at Nicol' alongside the locals, he was forced to admit that his features and stature were to say the least remarkably like theirs.

To the group's amazement, they were then manacled with balls and chains. They could walk only if two men carried the iron balls between them. They were taken to the nearby town, followed by an angry crowd of civilians gesticulating and shouting at them. "What are they saying?" the men asked Nicol'. He grinned wryly. "They are saying that we are spies and that we will be executed when we reach the town." On arriving at the town they were met by a senior officer who told them. " We know you're the men who blew up the aqueduct. You are convicts who have volunteered to train as parachutists in order to be released from prison in England." He called them "English desperadoes." The men were then hustled to a lorry and driven to the nearby railway station at Calitri. Before boarding the train the men were lined up and a fascist officer informed them "Tomorrow you will be shot at dawn. You are spies." Later, when the group had been handed over to the Italian military, an Italian general addressed them. "You were parachuted into the heart of Italy and have committed an act of sabotage. Your superiors must have known that you would never escape. At worst you would have been killed trying and at best you would have been taken as prisoners of war. A soldier myself, I appreciate bravery in any man. I will make you my personal responsibility and see that you are treated with honour, as prisoners of war in accordance with international rules." The group were then given their first decent meal for three days.

'X' Troop after their capture

'X' Troop's next destination was Naples, where they were incarcerated in a civilian jail. Here they found the rest of the troop, who had also been captured trying to reach the rendezvous on the coast. At first they were interrogated daily and constantly threatened with execution, but as the days went on the men stopped taking the threats seriously. Nicol' was constantly harassed about his Italian appearance and the fact that he spoke in the local dialect. It was a bad day for them when one of the interpreters was taken from the camp and did not return. Later the men heard to their horror that he had been executed because he admitted that he was Italian and proud of it, but that he loathed and detested fascism.

Concern for Nicol' grew among the men. There was no doubt that the Italians were highly suspicious of his background. Eventually they unravelled the anagram 'Tristan' and came up with 'Nastri'. They searched the area for families of the same name, and found a family who admitted to having a relative in England. This was indeed the sister of Alfonso senior, Nicolo's aunt. They brought the Signora to Naples and confronted her with Nicol', and said, "You know this man, don't you? – he is a relative of yours." She answered. " I have never seen this man before." "You know him, he is your nephew, the son of your brother in England," they insisted. His aunt looked him straight in the eye, and announced, "I have never seen this man before, my nephew in England is a sickly youth, always ill. He is nothing like this man." The interrogators turned to Nicol'. "You know this woman? She is your father's sister." He addressed his aunt: "Never seen you in my life before, Missus. Clear off!" She narrowed her eyes and, staring at him, she hissed, "*Bastardo!*" Nicol' said later that he never loved his aunt more than at that moment. His Aunt Adele had saved his life by denying him. In later years, whenever Nicol' returned to Ravello, he always took his Aunt Adele a special present.

Months later the group were transferred to Campo di Concentramento 78 at Sulmona, a prisoner-of-war camp in the mountains of Abruzzo. Although conditions in the camp were severe and for a time the group were segregated from the other prisoners, intervention by the Red Cross led to their being moved into the main compound, where conditions were better. It was during this period that the Nastri family received their first communication from their son. Later another telegram was received from Bern saying that the Vatican had transmitted a list of names of the men who had taken part in the raid. Unfortunately the family never heard the broadcast, as their radio had been confiscated.

In 1943 the allied invasion of Sicily began and the allies were advancing north. It wasn't long before Italy capitulated, whereupon the guards simply opened the gates of the camp, telling the men they were free and they could either stay put and wait for the advancing allies, or they could make their way south to meet them. With several others Nicol' decided to make for the surrounding hills, where they joined up with the local partisans. They were welcomed with open arms. On account of his skills as a trained commando and his knowledge of the local dialect, Nicol' was soon made Captain. Under his command the group would harass German convoys by throwing Molotov cocktails at lorries as they made their way through the mountain passes. The local farmers in the area welcomed the partisans into their homes and they were welcomed at the *festas* (Saints' feast days) held in the surrounding villages.

One mission too far saw them captured by the Germans. Nicol' recounted to Victor his memory of the moments before his capture, whilst fleeing from his pursuers. The sound of bullets hitting the ground at his heels as he ran was the most frightening experience he had throughout the whole operation. Now they were prisoners of the Germans. On a goods train heading for Germany they made another bid for freedom. As they approached the Brenner Pass there was an air-raid warning and the train stopped. The men prised up the floor boards of the truck and dropped onto the tracks. They decided to try and make it to the Yugoslav border. Once again they were on the run, but not for long. They were soon recaptured and Nicol' spent the rest of the war in a camp at Innsbruck. It was during this period that he was injured. He refused to work on Christmas day and a guard struck him across the head with the butt of his rifle. The resulting operation entailed the insertion of a metal plate into his skull. This was the only injury that Nicol' sustained throughout the whole of Operation Colossus.

Nicol' was 19 years old at the start of the war and 23 by the time he returned home. What an experience for a boy from Little Italy. Operation Colossus was rated as one of the most daring exploits of WW II. The group all received citations or medals, among them the DSO, the MC, and the MM. Trooper Nastri was mentioned in despatches in recognition of 'Gallant and Distinguished Service in the Field' and he was awarded the 'Oak Leaf.'

Cavaciuti family –
the 'ice cream boys'

The following story was sent to me in 1987 by Andrea (Andy) Cavaciuti, who was then living in Manhattan, New York.

Born on 16 April 1897 in Rusteghini, Morfasso (Piacenza), my father, Antonio Cavaciuti, was no different from any other hard-working Italian. He was a proud man with the need and desire to provide the best he could for his family, and in doing so he left Italy and eventually became a part of the community in Clerkenwell known as Little Italy.

Life there was never smooth, indeed at times quite bumpy, but it appeared to offer more than he had left in Rusteghini. Before he was able to work in his own profession, mosaic and terrazzo making, he worked (like many other Italians) in the collieries in Wales, where he also served 15 months in the third Battalion of the Welsh Fusiliers.

Finally he returned to Italy to marry his sweetheart of many years, Caterina Bellini. They returned to Wales as a family of three (I was the third) in 1924. On 24 May 1925 they moved to Clerkenwell where they found rooms at No.24 Leicester Place, a small mews off Little Saffron Hill, opposite the Italian School. Additions to the family prompted further moves, finally to No.29 Calthorpe Street, where we stayed for many years. The children grew up as part of the Italian community, attending St Peter's Italian School, whose playgrounds were the streets; many times we ran home at playtime only to be dragged back to school by an angry mother. At weekends we would collect empty wooden boxes which I would chop up and cart around the houses, selling to housewives for the grand sum of a penny a sack.

At school we had good teachers but, for the most part, we were not the best students and had many an ear pulled, not to mention the whackings. Sport was another matter. In the main we excelled at football and athletics. In those days, there were many Italian ice cream vendors in London, so when we played football against other schools, we were always referred to as 'the ice cream boys'. Despite the many bumps along the road, we all survived. We all had plenty of determination and the ambition to improve ourselves, inherited, of course, from our parents who took the first step by leaving the land of their fathers.

World War I changed all of our lives in the Italian community in London. My father, despite having served in the Welsh Fusiliers in World War II, was interned and put on the Arandora Star. He was one of the few survivors who, having been in a rowing boat for 5 days, were picked up by a Canadian destroyer, the St Laurent, and taken back to Liverpool. From there they were taken in another ship to Australia for the duration of the war.

At 14 I had started work in the Hanover Restaurant, but when I was 16 I too was interned: I was the only Cavaciuti son to be born in Italy and my parents had never changed my nationality because they still held property in Italy. We all thought of ourselves as Italian; only in wartime did it matter who was born in Italy. The worst part of the internment was initially being mixed with German internees in the camp near London: they would cheer as German planes passed overhead on their bombing raids, while we, with families remaining in London, prayed. Eventually we Italians were sent to the Isle of Man, leaving the Germans in Shropshire.

My mother struggled in those difficult times, raising the younger children alone while her breadwinners were interned, not even together. But the war eventually ended, we returned to our family and were once more a part of Clerkenwell. I wonder if the present generation of Italians living in London or New York realise just how much courage and fortitude it took simply to survive in those early years.

Clerkenwell will always have special memories for me, and as I look back I fondly recall the annual procession, St Peter's Italian School, the Italian Church, the clubs, Exmouth Street Market, the people I grew up with, the Malvesi family, with their café at the end of Calthorpe Street, the Azzali brothers, the De Luca family, Rospo and many others.

My parents, Antonio and Caterina, died several years ago at 29 Calthorpe Street. My brothers and sisters still live on there, simply moving from No.29 to No.31 next door.

In 1953 I married an English girl, Mary King. We emigrated to the USA, where for several years I had a restaurant in Manhattan, which had to close when the lease expired. I have since joined my wife in business and we import Mexican specialities – fruits, vegetables and spices. We have one son who married an American girl, Mary Seigler.

We have become a typical American family, but, in reminiscing, the one thing I have always enjoyed is to return in memory to 'The Hill' and have a drink with the old boys at the Coach & Horses in Warner Street.

Antonio Mancini, 'Sharamagila'

The story is told by Mrs Ida Ermini née Fama

My family were one of the first to settle in the area known as "the Hill."
My grandfather Antonio Mancini came to London as an emigrant, and,
as far as we know, in 1855. As was usual down the Hill, he was rarely called by his
real name, but as Sharamagila, his nickname.

Like so many other Southern Italian residents of the Hill, he made his living
by selling ice cream from an ice cream cart in the streets. He had a regular pitch
outside Somerset House in the Strand. My grandmother, also a Southerner, was
called Maria Luisa.

They lived at No.2 Summer Street and here my grandmother gave birth to
eight children: only five survived childhood, including my mother, Maria Theresa.
My uncles never followed their father into the ice cream trade. They were barbers,
but each of them was also a talented musician. *Zio* (Uncle) Gus was an excellent
accordionist, whilst *Zio* Angelo played with the famous 'Troyes and his Mandolins'.

My grandfather was famous in the community because, with his friend
Enrico Voltrona, he used to go from house to house on Christmas Eve welcoming
the birth of the Saviour with traditional Italian tunes. Enrico played the flute and
my grandfather played a sort of bagpipe called a zampogna. (It was from this
instrument that the wandering minstrels of the Christmas season got their name,
I Zampognani.) Their visits to the households down the Hill were eagerly awaited.
The children, especially, looked forward to their coming and would follow them
from house to house.

My mother married Salvatore Fama, another Southerner – from Catania
(Sicily). He had arrived in the community around 1900 and started his working life
as a lather boy in one of the barbers' shops down the Hill. He would lather up the
customers ready for the barber's expertise with the cut-throat razor. The barbers'
shops were always busy because men who could afford it were shaved daily.

In time my father Salvatore was running his own shop, but his real love was
singing and accompanying himself on the guitar. He originally sang and played for
his own pleasure, or that of his family and friends. Eventually his talent as a singer
was recognised and he finally made it as a professional, singing with the famous
Mantovani and his Tipica Orchestra.

The early days for my family were extremely hard, there were five children,
but as most of our neighbours lived in similar circumstances, this helped. We lived
at No.16 Eyre Street Hill. The house was dilapidated, little more than a slum. The

landlords were more interested in collecting money than paying for repairs. Our rooms were kept as clean as humanly possible, but it was an uphill struggle. When it rained we had to put up umbrellas in an attempt to keep the rooms dry. We were pretty poor: I am not ashamed to say that there was a time when we had to break up our old chairs to use as fuel for the fire.

One of my earliest memories, when we lived at No.16, was of being awakened very early on summer mornings by the noise from the courtyard below, as the ice cream vendors prepared the ice cream, ready for the daily trudge around the streets of the city. The eggs and vanilla would have been boiled up the night before and left overnight. In the early hours the freezing process began. This was a noisy operation; sleep was impossible. To some extent this wasn't a bad thing, because no-one possessed an alarm clock and it was only by shouting down to the vendors below that we could find out the time, even if it was only 4 am.

My memories of my childhood down the Hill are nevertheless for the most part happy ones. True, life for a young girl was very restrictive. It was the girls' responsibility to help *Mamma* around the house – the boys had no such responsibilities. However, life wasn't all work and we usually found time to enjoy ourselves, gossiping and taunting the local boys. There were high spots in the year, especially Procession Sunday, a day when everything seemed special. On that day we were actually allowed to talk to, and dance with, the boys we had been taunting all the year – all under *Mamma's* or someone else's watchful eye.

My most precious memory amongst those days of deprivation came when King Victor Emmanuel II and his queen Elena came to the Italian Church (1935 or 1936) while on a rare visit to London. I managed to get through the crowds carrying a bouquet of flowers which I presented to the royal couple. It is funny how childish eyes are deceived, for I was convinced that the King was a big, tall man, whilst in reality he was quite small and short.

It makes me sad nowadays, walking around the area of the old Hill, to see it so empty and deserted.

Luisa Della Savina, née Ferrari ('Gigiola')

Luisa Ferrari was born in Borgo Val di Taro (Parma) in 1884. She was taken in by her mother's family of Della Savina when her mother died and her father remarried.

This story is not so much about the Della Savina family, but about Luisa. Her name was frequently mentioned, with a great deal of respect and affection, when ex-residents of 'The Hill' reminisced about the old days.

The family always treated Luisa as if she was one of their own. When she was 14 it was thought that she should go to London and work as a domestic for family friends, the Del Nevo family, who had migrated earlier and now had a small business in Finsbury Park.

On the channel crossing Luisa was very seasick; she was already homesick, and wondered what lay ahead for her. She was shedding tears when a young Italian, another emigrant from the village of Tiedoli in the same area, saw her distress and comforted her, dried her tears and made her laugh. Little did she realise at the time that the same young man, Giovanni Della Savina, was to be her future husband.

Luisa's early years in Finsbury Park were relatively happy; in the course of time Giovanni came back into her life, and 8 years after their first meeting on the ship they were married. After their first son Paul was born, they decided to try and make a new life in Paris, where they had relatives. They had another two children, Tony and Mary, during their time in France. For some reason, perhaps because WW I was about to erupt, England began to seem a safer haven for their young family.

1914 found the young family in rooms in Bath Street. Daughter Mary remembers going to the little nursery in Vine Street called Roding House. Her clearest memories are those of Procession Sunday; she remembers the excitement of the day and the smell of the *tortei* cooking and the tantalising aroma of salami mixed with the aromatic vapour of *insalata* based on *gruniard* (dandelion salad.) The clamour in the street as the decorations were put up, and the confusion that only Italians can create preceded every event of any moment.

She remembered the thrill of walking in her special outfit at some biblical event. She was quite aggrieved as she recalled one occasion when, as she was walking, her mind kept wandering back to the house and envisaging the fine fare that would be waiting. She rushed home as soon as the procession was over, only to find that numerous visitors had demolished every morsel of food. She chided her mother, who was well known for her hospitality: "What about us? You weren't thinking about us!"

The family remember clearly their years in Bath Street, the frequent knocking on their door, sometimes in the middle of the night, when their mother was called out by a neighbour, either because a baby was about to be born or someone had died. This courageous woman would hurry to the home in question and do whatever she could to help, even laying out the loved ones of her friends and neighbours. It seemed that anyone in a crisis would call on Gigiola. Gig', as she was affectionately referred to, worked for many years in Ted's café on the corner of Ray Street and Saffron Hill.

Gigiola holding her daughter Tina outside Ted's café

Ted Gasparo's café was a centre of activity and the meeting place for many of the male population of the quarter. Some of the asphalters would pick up their wages there. Friday would see the manager of the Excel Asphalt Company doling out the pay packets. He seemed to use the café as an office. Once the men had their pay some would repair to the Coach and Horses across the road for a drink, while others would settle for a cup of Gigiola's tea. The café boasted an open fireplace, and in the winter some of the older men would sit there for the best part of the day, drinking cups of tea, eating toast and chatting the hours away. All the regulars remembered Gigiola with affection for her kindness and patience, and there is no doubt that she would always listen to their troubles and do whatever she could to help them.

Many of the well-known characters in the locality were regulars in Ted's café, for instance, Nano Paradiso, who lived above Gella's, the little sweetshop-cum-grocers farther up Saffron Hill, opposite St Peter's School, as were Jimmy Falco and his friends. The place was always alive with activity, with young lads playing on the pinball machines and children running in and out all day for ice creams.

Like many of their compatriots the Della Savinas moved several times, either because of an increase in family numbers or in search of improved accommodation. Their first move from Bath Street was in the late 1920s, to a large block of dwellings on the fringe of the quarter, Victoria Dwellings, a triangular block on the corner of Clerkenwell Road, Farringdon Road and Ray Street. In Victoria Dwellings each flat was self-contained; on one side there were flats with their own sinks and toilets, albeit leading off the kitchen. On the other side of the building the toilets and sinks were outside the flats, on the stairwells and landings, and were shared by several families. These flats were preferable to rooms in overcrowded tenement houses and over the decrepit shops in the heart of the quarter, partly on account of the privacy they offered their occupants. Several families had seven, even ten, children, not only Italians but English and Irish too. The advantage for them was the yard in the inner triangle, where the children could play in relative safety.

Luisa Della Savina ('Gigiola')

The Della Savinas moved on from the dwellings a short distance down Little Saffron Hill to Leicester Place, a small, cobble-stoned courtyard opposite St Peter's Italian School. One family already living in their new house was the Fassini family, greatly respected in the community. No.2 Leicester Place was owned by Signor Luigi Viazzani (p 31). Apart from the Fassinis most of the tenants were transient lodgers, but these were soon replaced by regular tenants, smaller Italian families: the Ferraris, the Maestranzis and the Beltramis, all families from the Trentino region.

Gigiola as many would have known her

Giacinto and Albina Belli with their two sons also lived in No.2. Their eldest son Giovanni (Johnny) was to feature largely in the Della Savina home, as he courted and married Gigiola's youngest daughter, Tina. Those two sons, Giovanni and Roberto, are still active today in the celebration of the Procession. Gigiola's flat in No.2 had a capacious and comfortable kitchen. A large black range, which radiated a wonderful warmth, was a prominent feature. Indeed, such a cosy atmosphere prevailed in the room that there was always a lonely neighbour, a passing acquaintance or someone seeking a haven, seated by the stove; interminable cups of coffee were on offer and very often a plate of *minestra*. If the family complained about the constant flood of visitors, Gigiola's reply would always be: "Eh, *povrain* (poor things, dialect for *poverini*), what else can they do?"

The 1930s were contented years for the family. Papa was working in the kitchens of the Carlton Hotel, the older boys were employed and Mary was helping out at the Coach and Horses, where the proprietors, Netta and Lou Resteghini, treated her more like the daughter they had never had, than an employee. One of Mary's tasks was to keep an eye on young Nino, the couple's only son, and she would occasionally help out in the bar. Gigiola loved a party, and on festive occasions the large, cosy kitchen would vibrate to the sound of the accordion playing an old fashioned waltz or 'one-step'. The family's friends would all be in evidence and Gig' would be spun round the room by old family friends such as Daniso Molinari (taking time off from his card sessions down at Lou's public house), executing a traditional spinning waltz, to the strains of the old tunes like *La Spagnola*, sung no doubt with great gusto along with that other all-time favourite, *Mazzolin di Fiori*, and all the other nostalgic songs so loved by the *paesani*.

In 1940 Italy entered WW II. One evening a loud knocking at the door of No.2 sent Papa hurrying up the stairs to see what was amiss. On the step were two policemen. He realised immediately what was about to happen and the shock caused him to suffer a facial stroke (palsy). That night Giacinto Belli and his son Johnny were taken from the house to the local police station, registered as aliens to be interned and sent to the Isle of Man, where they were detained for 4 years. They were eventually allowed to have family visits. Albina went to see her husband and son on one or two occasions and Tina Belli, who was now in her early teens, went with her to keep her company.

The Della Savina family, like thousands of others, carried on with their lives in spite of the incessant air raids. When the sirens wailed they would hurry round to the side entrance of St Peter's Church in Back Hill and down into the cellars beneath the church, where bunks had been installed. Here with other families they felt safer, probably because of their close proximity to the church. In spite of the intense bombing, the hundreds of incendiary bombs that rained down on the capital, life went on. There was a lull when everyone began to breathe a little easier, but not for long. To the dismay of exhausted Londoners came another horror, the flying bomb – pilotless aircraft known officially as the V1. These terrifying objects destroyed 2,300 homes in London alone, but worse was to come. the V2 long-range rocket.

On 10 March 1945, at 11.10 am, a massive explosion shook the area for miles around. Minutes later Mary, who was working behind the bar at the Coach and Horses, saw her brother Paul rush into the bar. "Come quickly," he cried, "that landed in Smithfield and Mum's down there". They ran in the direction of the meat market, where they came upon Gigiola, blood streaming down her face from a head wound, walking away from the scene of devastation, dazed and unsteady and repeating, "That poor woman, she's *incinta* (pregnant), oh, that poor woman". She was referring to the young woman who had been serving her in Smith's butchers at the moment of impact. Paul and Mary wanted one thing: to get their mother to a hospital, but she was adamant. "There are lots of them worse off than me. Oh, those poor people, all lying there, a lot of them dead. The poor things, oh, those poor people". Gigiola in her usual caring way put the sufferings of others before her own pain.

The incident that happened on that day was almost the last rocket incident of the war. The figures were horrendous: 110 dead and 123 injured. The family managed to persuade Gigiola to go to the hospital the following day, where they simply dressed the wound in her head. No X-rays were taken and there were no further investigations – no doubt due to the pressure on the hospital's resources and the strain on the staff as they dealt with the vast number of casualties brought in the day before.

Gigiola was obsessed by the suffering she saw on that day and she couldn't

Luisa Della Savina ('Gigiola')

Scene in Smithfield market after V2 attack, 1945

get it out of her mind. She began to suffer terrible headaches. Her husband Giovanni, her family and friends were devastated when she died suddenly, aged 61, on 21 June 1945, from compression on the brain brought on by the injury she received on that dreadful day in Smithfield.

When the news of her death reached Borgo Taro, her relatives and friends there also felt the loss of her passing. She had never forgotten her roots and had returned home whenever possible between the wars, and she never failed to send parcels.

Francesco Lurati

The Artist

Francesco Lurati was never a resident in the Italian Quarter. His home was in Highbury, where he attended the nearest Catholic School, Our Lady and St Joseph's, in Tottenham Road, Dalston. His many connections with the Italian Church and the evening classes in St Peter's Italian School, which he attended daily after day-school, justify his inclusion in our stories of 'Little Italy.'

Francesco's father was the artist responsible for the two paintings that adorn the side altars of St Peter's Italian Church. Francesco himself is a brilliant artist and diarist, and among his diaries is a complete record of his days in the internment camps. Not only did he leave a written record, but he painted beautifully detailed watercolours and sketches of the interior and exterior of every location of his incarceration during those troubled times. He was only 17 years old when it began.

Here is Francesco's story:

I was born on 19 September 1919. At the age of 8 I enrolled for evening classes in the *Scuola Serale di San Pietro* (St Peter's Evening Classes) in Herbal Hill. Our day school ended at 4.30 pm and after school I would stop on my way to the Italian Quarter at a shack on the corner of Ball's Pond Road, to get sustenance before taking the tram to Laystall Street. This consisted of a crisp roll oozing with butter and real ham cut from the bone, and a cheesecake almost as big as my head, dripping with coconut, plus a large cup of tea, all for about sixpence. The *Diretrice della Scuola* (Headmistress) was Signorina Balestreri (see p 19), tall, with dark curly hair, and very dignified. The other teachers were Signorina Belli, a plump little lady, fair-haired and with an 'Eton crop' and a pert little nose like a sparrow; and Signorina Nizzoli, pale face, with straight black 'bobbed' hair.

There was also the 'Maestro' Ferrari (p 19), like a bird of prey, an eagle perhaps. He was tall, round-shouldered, a purplish red nose on which perched a pair of 'pince-nez' spectacles. On his head he wore an embroidered velvet skull-cap. Under his arm he carried his bacchetta (cane), always at the ready! I still have my *Medaglia d'Argento* (silver medal). I must have just missed being Best Boy.

Evening classes finished at 7.30 pm. I took the tram to Ball's Pond Road and was able to complete my walk home. Even in the dark it was quite safe for a child to roam abroad in those days. This was my first introduction to the Italian Community. The next step was to be enrolled as an Altar Server. There were about

40 of us in those days, ranging from little boys to grown men. My brother, Eugenio, at 3, was 'Boat Boy', that is, he carried the incense for the thurifer. At that time there was polished linoleum on the Sanctuary floor. Eugenio left his place to join the torch bearers on his first Sunday, skidded across the floor and landed on his bottom! We wore lace-trimmed cottas over purple cassocks on feast days, when the Sanctuary was a forest of flowers, potted palms and candles. Six crystal chandeliers hung from the ceiling with about fifty candles apiece. The machinery for lowering the chandeliers – wires and winches – is still above the Sanctuary ceiling.

On one occasion, when I was on the opposite side of the Sanctuary, I noticed that my little brother's face was becoming redder and redder, the tears starting to roll down his cheeks. He had been told to "be a good boy" and was afraid to move even though, in the heat, a few candles in the chandelier above him had bent over and were dripping hot wax on to his head. I took him into the Sacristy and endeavoured to comb the congealed wax from his hair.

Among the altar servers were also the Terroni brothers – Luigi and Pip, sons of Cavaliere Raffaele (p 104), a pillar of the community. Cavaliere Terroni looked outstanding in his winged collar and always very dignified, even during the many years of our shared internment during the war. Terroni's storeroom was somewhere in the bowels of the earth under the church, and appetising aromas of salami, cheeses and wine seeped up through the floorboards of St Joseph's altar, blending with the scented smoke of the thurible.

The third natural progression was to join the *Fascio*. I became a *Balilla*, then an *Avanguardista*, surprising all and sundry by becoming a musician in the band called the Fanfara di Londra. We took part in all the processions and I recall marching with the band down Eyre Street Hill, where the little houses would be decorated with altars and coloured lights at the windows and baskets of rose petals strung across the road. The baskets were pulled open by cords as the statue of the Madonna del Carmine or Santa Lucia passed beneath and they showered down their perfumed contents whilst white doves fluttered off to the rooftops or settled on windowsills. After the procession there would be lemonade and sticky buns at the old school hall. The policemen came down also, and they were regaled with beer.

The Fanfara di Londra had its hours of glory also. In 1929 we went to Italy to play during the *Colonie Estive* (summer camp), when we played in the piazzas of Viareggio, Cervia and Cattolica. Outside Viareggio, I remember, our camp was pitched in the *pineta* (pine forest). We used to go into the *pineta* to practise. Someone was sure to make a mistake. Maestro Fontauzza would tap his music-stand for us to stop. He would go over to the offending player and get immersed in sorting out the difficulty. When he turned to continue with the *prova* the clearing was empty; we had all scattered into the forest to pick blackberries. He had first to find Valvona, then get him to sound the *Adunata*. We would filter back and our *prova* would continue – until the next false note.

On Christmas Eve 1992, my family and I arrived early at St Peter's for

Midnight Mass and I sat next to Giovanna (Servini) Cardetti. We reminisced about the days of yore. I mentioned Signorina Belli and, to my amazement, was told that she used to lodge with Giovanna's family and that Giovanna was still in touch with her. My very first Italian teacher still drove her car at the age of 91 and was a universally loved and respected citizen of her native Bardi. I still have a postcard dated 15 October 1930. It reads: "St Peter's School, *La Scuola Italiana rincominciata. Prego presentersi il più presto possibile - le iscrizioni, salvo scuse eccezionali, terminano oggi - G Belli.*" (The Italian School is restarting. Please present yourself as soon as possible. Registration, unless there are exceptional reasons, will end today. G Belli.)

Lurate Abbate is a '*frazione*' (hamlet) above Lake Como. Some time in the distant past a family from this little haven moved down into Ponte Chiasso and they became known as I Lurati. Here in the ancestral home my great-grandfather, Giovanni Lurati, was born in 1821. He had two sons and a daughter. One of his sons, Giuseppe Antonio, my grandfather, was born on 5 March 1852. The picture of the old house in via Brogeda was painted by my father in 1930. Just behind the house was 'Il Rete', the chain fence that defined the frontier with Switzerland. There was also a lake with an island in the middle.

In 1869, at 17, my grandfather arrived in London. Unlike many of our emigrants, Giuseppe had a job waiting for him with Signor Corti, a family friend who had emigrated earlier and was already established as a manufacturer of artificial flowers. His next job was with the Salvias, in the same trade, at 117 Pitfield Street, Hoxton.

Even in those days there was moonlighting: he also worked behind the bar in Gatti's Music Hall in Villiers Street, Strand [see *Continental Taste*, CHS 1997]. It is now the Player's Theatre. Walter Salvia told me that he was the best worker they had ever employed. He was also, he said, "quite a tough guy". If there was ever trouble at Gatti's he didn't waste time going round the counter but would jump over the top, straight into the fray. It was here that he met Martha Durham, my grandmother. She had a small scar on her nose, a souvenir of an evening when, during a fracas, bottles and glasses started to fly. I like to think that *Nonno* rescued this damsel in distress and carried her off to the altar.

Their son, my father, another Giuseppe Antonio, was born on 1 July 1882; his sister, Aunt Giuseppina, on 10 December 1903. His old employer, Signor Corti, had returned to Chiasso with his English wife, Anna Ellis, for a happy retirement. The natives of Chiasso always referred to him as L'Inglese (The Englishman).

My father Giuseppe would tell me stories of how, with his sister Giuseppina, he would wander round Hoxton Market, sturdily protected by their pet bulldog. The market runs parallel to Pitfield Street where my *Nonno* worked. Later, the family moved to Southwark and my father attended the school attached to Southwark Catholic Cathedral. Occasionally he would accompany his father to work at Gatti's, where he would amuse himself behind the scenes trying on the artists' costumes.

Nonno died in 1905 at the age of 53. He suffered from asthma, probably brought on by the atmosphere of the artificial-flower workshops, full of powdered dyes and *farina* (potato flour) used for stiffening flower petals etc.

At the age of 14 my father started work at the City Sandblast Company in New North Road, where he created designs which were sandblasted on to frosted glass windows used in public houses. From there he found his way into the firm of T B Brown, an advertising agency in Upper Thames Street, and eventually went freelance. He became the artist for 'Clarnico' (Clarke, Nicholls and Coombes) and Pascall's, both confectioners. He designed chocolate and sweet boxes, sweet jars and wrapping for the contents. Another of his clients was Tom Smith's who were, I believe, the originators of Christmas crackers. Apart from boxes, he designed little stick-on motifs of figures and flowers which children used to collect and stick in their scrapbooks.

My father met Christine Pitts as St Monica's Church, Hoxton. They were married on his 30th birthday, 1 July 1912. Their first home was in Noel Road, Islington. Then they moved to the top-floor flat and attics of 99 Grosvenor Road, Highbury, where my sisters Agnes, Theresa and Margherita were born. WW I was in progress, in fact Margherita was born during an air raid. Beneath the rear windows of 99 Grosvenor Road is the railway and Canonbury Station. During the war the ammunition trains rumbled up and down, so my father beat a hasty retreat to 48 Beresford Street, Highbury, where the rest of the family were born: Francesco, Veronica, Benito, Maria and Eugenio.

There was some suggestion that, to avoid being called up, my father might be able to claim Swiss nationality – he only had to delete the 'Ponte' from Ponte Chiasso. However, looking down the list of options, and with his ever-growing family in mind, he noticed that the best-paid job in the forces was that of stoker in the British Navy. He volunteered, but they wouldn't let him have even a sniff at the rum ration – he had an Italian name! In any case it is certain that he wouldn't have lasted a day down in the fiery depths of the hold of a warship. He spent his army days in France in the trenches, painting crosses for the victims and putting names and company insignia on the memorials. Even during the war, when on leave, he still did work for Clarnico and continued after the war under contract to them.

With the war behind him he returned home to his wife and three little girls, Agnese, Teresa and Margherita. His parents celebrated the armistice with the birth of Francesco (me).

My father, self-taught as an artist by frequent visits to the library in Holloway Road, mastered watercolours, oil painting, tempera (colours mixed with egg white), portraits, etching, lithography, wood carving, fresco painting (painting on fresh plaster) – almost every technique of art. Although born here in England, he was ardently drawn towards Italy, cradle of his religion and his art.

He encouraged me to learn a poem. I recall the first stanzas:

L'esole colle, lontano sull' orizzonte
Ove, tingendo di Rosa il Monte,
Pur ora il sole nel mar discese
È il mio Paese
Vorrei posarmi coll'aura molle
Sui primi fiori del natio colle

Baciar con dolce malinconia
La terra Mia
Il tempio e l'ara ove primiera
Feci al Signore la prima preghiera
È come puro raggio di stella
L' alba era bella

(The lonely hill far away on the horizon as
   the sun sinking down over the sea
Reddens the mountain that is my homeland.
I would like to lie down and rest,
Among the first flowers brushed by a gentle
   breeze from the hills where I was born,

And kiss my homeland with sweet
   melancholy.
The church and the altar
   where I said my first prayer.
My soul was then as beautiful
   as the starlight.)

In our garden in Beresford Road, Highbury, Papa built a swing decorated with trellis work, and a seesaw. But the street was the great attraction with all the other girls and boys – and the games: skipping, cricket, football, whipping tops, marbles and conkers, various games played with cigarette cards – all had their seasons.

I went to Italy for the first time in 1929, with the *Colonie Estive*. The *Fascio* at that time was at 98 Great Russell Street, by the British Museum. We lined up outside in the road and marched to Victoria Station to entrain at 10 pm. My father and some of my sisters, with other families, came along. I was particularly glad of this because Papa carried my rucksack.

We were two nights and three days on the train The train chugged through Belgium, France, Germany and Switzerland, picking up boys and girls from the various towns. The train became longer and longer, engines at front, centre and back. Between the carriages there were observation platforms, open, like verandas, so that one could feel part of the countryside.

At about 5 am on the second morning we arrived at Chiasso. The sun was not up and it was a cold grey morning. In a daze, I heard "Lurati" being called up and down the platform. I peered out of the window and became aware of a crowd of people calling for ME! Upwards of fifty relatives: from Papa's *Zio* Eugenio, 81 years old, down to cousin Flaviano, 4 years old, in a black velvet suit with a frilly blouse. Cousin Giulio, 10 years my senior, lifted me down from the high carriage window, because the doors were locked.

When I arrived home in London, I was greeted with: "We have a surprise for you!" "What is it?" "Something live." "A rabbit? Where is it?" "Upstairs.".
I went up to my parents' bedroom and there was a little brother, Eugenio! This was the first that I knew of what was happening. Some years before, in 1926, my bed was normally by the side of my parents'. One night I was aware of a bit of a stir and my bed was moved to the far corner of the room, behind the washstand. In the morning I woke to find that Maria had joined our happy band, on 2 February, Candlemas Day.

Internment - excerpts from the diary of Francesco ('La Mia Guerra')

Sunday 9 June 1940 at St Peter's Italian Church: Delfina, who was to become my wife, had come from Stoneleigh to meet me for the 11 am mass. I served the altar and later we went over to the Mitre, a little 16th-century pub just off Hatton Garden. We then spent a happy day at her home. As I reluctantly left her to return to London on the last train to Waterloo I never dreamt that there would follow such a long and bitter separation. I was optimistic, she less so. Tuesday 11 June: I was at my place of work (a job advertised in the *Catholic Times* for the sons of Catholic gentlemen to train as buyers in a ladies' fashion house). Asked to come to the manager's office for a moment, I found two strangers who handed me a paper. I was under arrest. A letter written in Italian by Delfina, found in my pocket as they searched me, became vital evidence against me. I was taken home where three other men had searched the house, then crushed into a car with a total of five hefty plain-clothes policemen. I was taken to Upper Street Police Station, then, later that evening, to Brixton Prison, where I was questioned as to my criminal past and bunged into a dirty, smelly reception cell, then called out to join a queue of other unfortunates – friends and acquaintances.

After being stripped and searched we were led to cells in F Wing. Keys rattled, cell doors slammed. Next morning what an amusing, though unpleasant scene, to see men and boys of all social ranks trotting up and down carrying with half-averted eyes their new *insignia offici* (badge of office) ... a brimming chamber-pot. We were locked up for 22 hours a day, we were harangued by the chief officer. No whistling, no singing, no anything. We were allowed two letters a week and a sheet of paper on which to make our 'appeal.' I was so politically innocent that I made my 'appeal' against regulation 13B – considering my situation, an appropriate unlucky number. It should of course have been 18B, the regulation that put habeas corpus on ice, and allowed the government to detain anyone for more than 15 days without charge or trial. On Friday we were taken to the Prison Chapel, bristling with police, to hear Mass. There were many shoulders shaking with silent sobs as familiar hymns were intoned.

I received a welcome visit from my parents - told them to urge Delfi to try and get a visiting pass. We began to settle down, even here. But this was shortlived. On Saturday morning we were awakened by a beating on the cell doors and cries of "Get up – you're going out." Vans awaited us outside the prison. I had hoped to drop a hastily scribbled note to my parents – not a dog's chance. More police than prisoners. We entrained at Euston and eventually discovered that we were bound for Liverpool, and landed in Walton jail! Ten times more menacing than Brixton, there followed the usual initiation strip search, 'medical exam' (down with the trousers, up with the shirt,) through crashing doors and gates to B Wing, which had been uninhabited for 20 years – dust and filth everywhere. My turn came. Cell B3 11 (B Wing, Landing 3, Cell 11.) The door shut with a slam that nearly blew my brains out. I threw myself on the mattress, my head in a whirl. I made an effort,

Francesco Lurati

jumped up and started to walk up and down, a distance of six paces, reciting the Rosary on my fingers, praying to have the courage to cope with this turn of events. For 10 days we were left with nothing but the clothes we wore, not even a piece of soap with which to wash. I did my best to wash and clean my abode with a piece of sacking and a bucket of cold water. The food was foul.

31 July 1940: on the move again, this time to Camp 007, Ascot, Berkshire. At least it was in the open air. The camp had been the winter quarters for Bertram Mills' circus animals, but we were a poor substitute for noble lions and majestic elephants. I was among the last to be allocated accommodation, with Toni Molinari (banker), Avvocato De Reya (lawyer) and a half dozen other youngsters. Rations, very meagre, were issued to be cooked by ourselves in the kitchens. I used to go to the kitchen window for the cabbage water in which floated various well cooked insects, adding to the protein. Salted herrings figured largely in the diet - inedible. Eventually a little priest came to say Mass at our outside altar, made of benches covered with blankets. Poor little man, he was quite nervous to start with – thought we were going to eat him! We could have done with an extra bit of meat. However, when he got to know us he relaxed. We asked permission of Captain Petrie to have confession. He replied: "I don't care if you petition the Pope – we're not interested." He had to give in eventually and apologised for the irreverent remark.

19 September 1940: My 21st birthday – but they didn't give me the key to the gates. 15 October 1940, Wednesday: My 'Tribunal,' a farce. Three grim-faced men sat in judgment. The first thing I noticed was that the chairman, Sir Roland Campbell QC, had a tuft of hair on the top of his nose. My crime: I had joined the *Fascio* at the age of 8 and I had been to Italy six times with the *Colonie Estive* to soak up the sun and culture. I tried to explain that I could not, would not, don a uniform to fight against my own people, but would be willing to do any humanitarian work. Verdict: join the army or stay where you are – until doomsday.

The next day, for a quarter of an hour, I had a fleeting visit from my darling Delfina. Hours of journeying for a fleeting 15 minutes!

28 October 1940: On the move again to Camp 003, "York Racecourse." Billeted under the grandstand, water dripping down the walls, turning to ice and frost as the winter drew on. One cold tap and two buckets behind a partition to pander to our bodily needs. 40 men were locked in this room from 4 pm to 8 am.

1 March 1941: On the move again to Camp 009, Huyton, Liverpool, an unfurnished council estate. The move to Huyton was strategic – it was near the sea. Since the days when criminals were transported to Australia for stealing a loaf of bread, a law had been passed to forbid the enforced moving of British subjects overseas. This was rescinded and, on 13 May 1941 I and a boatload of others found ourselves on the briny heading for the Isle of Man, destination Camp 'M,' Peel. The net of 18B had trawled a motley collection of men: Anglo-Italians, Anglo-Germans, members of Mosley organisations, even the son of a British Admiral and another chap who had taken out Haitian citizenship.

On the other side of the barbed wire there was a large pub called the Greg

Malin – we affectionately called it "the Kremlin." It was the military and drinking headquarters of our guards. Tension had been rising for weeks – no letters, no parcels, petty restrictions, no visits, and when three escapees were recaptured a few miles off the coast of Ireland and were refused food, *L'invasione Di Vasi (Da Notte)* ("The Charge of the Chamber Pots") took place. The Kremlin was bombarded over the wire with piles of chamber pots that were obtained from the cupboards of the boarding houses in which we were billeted (no "en suite" loos in those days.) It was great fun while it lasted. The Commandant was summoned

Francesco Lurati

Italian internees in Camp 'M', Peveril, Peel, Isle of Man, 1941

from Douglas, and the prisoners got their food.

Saturday, 24 January 1942: Many of the Italians who had fathers, brothers or relatives in Italian camps had asked to join them. So it was that I was transferred to Camp "N" where the atmosphere was *più simpatico* (more sympathetic).

Friday, 5 March 1943: They (MI5) have come up with what they call 'The New Scheme,' a form full of questions to kindle hope of release. One of the questions was: "What are your nicknames?" Cavaliere Terroni calls it "*Il Nuovo Complotto!*" (The New Conspiracy).

18 March 1944: Transferred to Camp "S," the Metropole at Douglas. I had refused to be herded around like an animal. I was taken to the cells and next morning transported under guard with two others to the new camp – at least we didn't have to carry our own baggage!

Thursday, 31 August 1944: Is it really true? I'm going home!

In 1945 I just skipped 'All Fools Day' and married Delfina Maria Rossotti, who had waited for me throughout the 4 years of my internment, and we lived "happily ever after."

Terroni family

One of the first delicatessen family businesses in the Italian Quarter

The 1912 wedding of Raffaele Terroni and Paola Maria di Falco. L to R: Maria Terroni (groom's mother), Giuseppe di Falco (bride's father), the bride, Letizia Terroni (bridesmaid), the bridegroom, Duilio Terroni (groom's youngest brother), Giovanni Terroni (groom's brother), Giovanni Terroni (groom's father)

At the age of 17 Luigi Terroni left the hamlet of Vesrada, in the mountains of Northern Italy just above Pontremoli near Massa Carrara, and headed on foot over the mountain passes to London. He arrived in Clerkenwell late in 1971, sleeping in one of the lodging houses and working so hard at unspecified jobs until he had enough to set up a shop in Summers Street selling Italian produce. After a few years he was able to return to Vesrada and marry his childhood sweetheart Caterina Terroni (no relation). On returning to England they lived in a little house in Warner Street, and produced ten children, of whom five survived: Giovanni born 1881, Roberto 1885, Raffaele 1890, Maria 1893, and Letizia 1895. Luigi opened a second shop, initially selling wine but later other Italian delicacies, at 138 Clerkenwell Road adjacent to the Italian Church and as they grew older Giovanni and Roberto worked in the business too.

In 1902 Luigi fell ill and Raffaele, the third son, had to leave school at 12 to help his older brothers in the two shops. Working for the family business meant working from dawn till dusk. As the firm grew, they employed other immigrants who were given lodgings in the rooms above the Summer Street shop.

As each of the children married they continued to live with their parents in the family home in Warner Street. When Raffaele was 22 he married a pretty little Neapolitan girl, Paola Maria di Falco, a union which no doubt helped mend the rift that existed then between Northerners and Southerners in Little Italy (the di Falcos were from Saviano, a small village on the outskirts of Naples). The young couple also moved in with the Terroni family and their first child, Caterina, was born there.

The whole family moved in 1914 to a large property on the corner of Little Bath Street (today Eyre St Hill) and Warner Street, Nos.32/34, spacious rooms above a warehouse, and stayed there for 27 years. Raffaele's second baby, Luisa, was born there in 1914. Then the shop in Summers Street and the rooms above were destroyed by a fire, one of the lodgers escaping only by jumping out of a top

The Terroni family in 1949/50. Back row L-R: Giuseppe (Pip), Antonio Ciccone, Angiola, Peter Di Giuseppe, Lu. Front row: Carolina holding Raphael, Caterina holding Gabriele, Raffaele, Paola Maria holding Paola, Luisa holding Peter, Bruna holding Stefanie.

floor window. The delicatessen was therefore transferred to Clerkenwell Road and combined with the wine shop. As it kept its stores under the church itself, Lurati (p 95) also recalls that fragrant aromas used to float up into the church to mingle with the smell of incense. "L Terroni & Sons" was familiar to all who lived in the Italian Quarter for many years.

During WW I the second son Roberto was conscripted into the British army, whereas after Italy joined the allies in 1915 Raffaele was sent to Italy to work as an interpreter, doing which he travelled the length and breadth of war-torn Northern Italy.

In 1917 Maria died at 24. Some members in the community remember going as children to see, and pray for, the beautiful young girl laid out in the family home. *Papa* Luigi died in the same year at the age of 64, and Giovanni, Roberto and Raffaele became equal partners in the family business. Paola undertook the arduous and dangerous journey, with her two little daughters Caterina and Luisa, to Italy in order to see her husband Raffaele. They stayed in Saviano with Paola's family and

Raffaele made his way down from the North for a joyous reunion with his wife and children. In September 1918 Luigi Terroni was born there, the only member of Raffaele's family to be born in Italy, and in 1919 the whole young family returned to 32/34 Warner Street. Giovanni, Roberto and Raffaele again ran the family shop.

More children were born in the 1920s: Giovanni had Duilio and Tarquinia (Queenie), Roberto produced Mario and Luigi. Letizia married Gaetano Petti and they had three sons, Vincent, Tony and Luigi. Raffaele and Paola had another child, Giuseppe (Pip).

Raffaele was deeply involved in the welfare of the community. Homesick new arrivals in the Quarter would go to the shop where Raffaele had a little office. There he would sort out their problems, interpret their mail, and write their letters for them. He often accompanied a troubled *paesano* to the courts, where he would help them with their legal and business matters. A large majority of the older residents could neither read or write; many of the women mixed only with the other inhabitants of the quarter, and in some cases, although they had lived in London for many years, they never learned to speak any English. In addition to his work for the Italian community, Raffaele was involved with St Peter's Italian Church for many years, was the Honorary Secretary of St Peter's Italian School and for The Italian Benevolent Society. In 1923 he was made Cavaliere (Corona d'Italia) by the Italian Government. Francesco Lurati remembers how distinguished Cavaliere Raffaele always looked, even when they were together in an internment camp.

Young Caterina remembered an incident that happened on a family holiday in Brighton. Raffaele was fishing on a jetty when a child playing nearby fell into the sea. Without hesitation Raffaele jumped into the water, grabbed the child and hung onto him until a boat came to the rescue. Paola and the children were playing farther along the beach. When Paola heard the commotion, she sent Caterina to investigate. Her daughter returned to say that Papa had been for a swim with all his clothes on and was receiving the attention of the first-aid people as he'd received a blow on the head from a rescue boat. He was taken to hospital, but it was only a minor injury and he was soon released. Later he was awarded a certificate from the Humane Society. The name of the little boy he rescued was John Tree and his father was so grateful to Raffaele that he gave him a silver-topped walking cane.

Young Luigi, Raffaele's son, recounts his boyhood memories of life in what to the outside world appeared to be a miserable area of unspeakable deprivation. "First and foremost" says Luigi "there was the great sense of belonging, being a part of one big family; the atmosphere that pervaded the streets was that of deep friendship, friendships that have been maintained for decades – long after the Italian Quarter ceased to exist." Lu would wake to the sounds of the 8 am hooter calling workers to the nearby Temple Press, and the clip-clop of the horses' hooves as they sped along pulling the carts that carried the Royal Mail along Warner Street, under the bridge to Mount Pleasant where the huge Sorting

Offices were. The Mail carts would go back and forth rattling along these narrow streets, all day and all night, adding to the cacophony of noise, as the fruit and veg traders pulled out their carts from the alleys and mews where they were housed overnight. "I heard the cries of "Buon giorno, amici," and the ice-cream vendors singing their national songs as they stirred their ice cream in the metal vats on their colourful barrows (see also p 14). Then there were the sounds of the organs from the factory just two doors up Little Bath Street, where Signor Chiappa, the famous manufacturer of organs, made everything from barrel-organs to the big organs that played on fairground roundabouts. As the morning went on there were the children running to St Peter's School, all calling out to one another, and the mothers in their various dialects shouting: "hurry, hurry, you will be late." In spite of the traffic, in their midday break and after school there would be football, twenty or so boys to a side, all chasing a ball made of newspaper rolled into a hard ball. The roads were their pitch, and jackets thrown down on the side of the road marked the goalposts."

Boys of all ages would join in the games: the elder Nastri Brothers, the Paradiso boys, Lu's younger brother, Pip. They saw no danger, as cars were few and they got plenty of warning of approaching horses and carts. Another of the youngsters' pastimes was to cross the road into Bath Court to visit the premises of Lazzero Cura, a naturalist, where they would be fascinated by the large tanks filled with tropical fish, frogs and reptiles.

"At the end of busy fun-filled days, I would go to sleep to the lullaby of the trams as they crossed over the bridge along Rosebery Avenue, and the noisy banter of the *baloche* (out-of-work teenagers) playing dice on the corner outside the house, mingling with the melodies of carousel music coming from Chiappa's workshop. No law decreed a starting and finishing time to the day's work in the Quarter. Businesses, however small, would work on until the last customer was served or the last order completed."

When Luigi was 9 Raffaele sent his two sons to the Salesian College in Battersea where they remained as day boys up to the age of 16. Lu went on from there to Clark's College in Chancery Lane where he took a two-year business course in shorthand, typing and book-keeping. This was the 1930s, a time of high unemployment, and foreigners were not welcome in white-collar jobs. Hard as Lu tried he was unable to get the type of job for which he was qualified, apart from a short spell with an insurance company in the City.

Meanwhile, brother Pip started out as an apprentice engineer in Leatherby's, a small business adjacent to St Peter's, but later went into the Civil Service (Trinity House), where he was employed for many years. He took lessons in music, painting and languages and became an excellent pianist, artist and linguist. In later years he was known as a fine teacher of music. In 1944 he married Carolina Di Giuseppe. They had three children, Raffaele, John and Maria. To his father's delight, one of his sons took to music and is now a successful concert pianist.

Giovanni, the eldest brother of the family, had never been robust and it was thought in 1924 that it would be best if he retired. His son, Duilio, now aged 16 and recently returned from a seminar in Italy, took his place in the shop, where he served for many years. He in his turn also served as Hon. Sec. of the Benevolent Society and he was also founder member and treasurer of the Mazzini-Garibaldi Club. In 1955 he was the second member of the family to be awarded the honour of *Cavaliere* for his work in the community.

Raffaele's wife, Paola Maria di Falco, had always been plagued with poor eyesight, despite which her fingers were always busy, plying her crochet hook.

Terroni girls carrying the statue of Santa Lucia (Giuseppe di Falco walking alongside)

Crochet is a skill that was taken for granted by families at that time. Italian homes even today, often have a piece of the exquisite work, an antimacassar or lace doily, that *Nonna* made and that has been handed down over the years. Paola Maria's father, Giuseppe di Falco, concerned about the deterioration of his daughter's eyesight, went to Italy where he had a statue of Santa Lucia (patron saint of the eyes) reproduced in life-size and sent to England. That same statue is the one that you can still see today being carried through the streets of Clerkenwell on Procession Sunday. In the early 1930s the statue was carried by young girls in the family, members of the 'Children of Mary'. The tableau was organised by di Falco, and as you can see in the photograph taken in 1936, he always walked alongside it.

In later years Raffaele took his place. Photographs of the procession show different generations of the Terroni family bearing the statue. As each generation ages, younger family members take over.

The mid-1930s saw improvements in the Italian Quarter. The depression was over and Italians were finding it easier to get jobs, mostly in catering, but also in the asphalt and terrazzo trades. Statuette makers had set up several small factories in the area, the biggest and best known being Pagliai in Goswell Road. The ice-cream trade was also booming. Londoners were beginning to regard the

Raffaele, Duilio, Roberto, Luigi and Giovanni Terroni with assistant Benedetto outside the delicatessen in the Clerkenwell Road

Italians with less suspicion, and the Italians were integrating and settling down.

But in 1935 Mussolini's invasion of Abyssinia set good relations back. There were a few racist flare-ups and cinema audiences booed when newsreels showed Italian tanks rolling into Abyssinia. The Terroni family business suffered from sanctions imposed on Italian imports that made 99% of their commodities unobtainable. They saved the business by replacing Italian goods with produce from Spain and Argentina.

Slum clearances in the Italian Quarter by the government moved some families living in over-crowded, insanitary conditions into blocks of council flats recently built in the surrounding areas. Along with several other families, mostly those with small businesses, pubs or clubs, the Terronis were happy to remain in 32/34 Warner Street. Duilio, Raffaele and Roberto were still running the business in Clerkenwell Road.

Raffaele's family

Paola Maria with her two daughters regularly returned to Saviano to visit relatives. On one of these trips Caterina (Rina) met the Neapolitan boy Antonio Ciccone. In 1937 Antonio came to London and the couple were married in St Peter's Italian Church. The date coincided with Raffaele and Paola Maria's silver wedding and there was a spectacular *festa speciale*.

Antonio had a good career ahead of him when they returned to Saviano. Starting out as a lawyer, he eventually became Head of Police. Their son Gabriele went like his father into Public Security, eventually becoming chief of the Flying Squad in Rome. Daughter Angela is a professor of Italian and philosophy. Rina never returned to England but lived to a grand old age in Saviano. She liked nothing better than to chat with her brother Luigi Terroni on the phone about the rest of the family in England, and to reminisce about the old days 'down the Hill'.

In 1938 the Munich Crisis saw the children of St Peter's school preparing for evacuation, but when Neville Chamberlain waved his piece of paper the *Mammas* heaved a sigh of relief, only to go through the whole thing again in September 1939, this time for real.

The Hill was quiet: the departure of the children and some of the *Mamma*s was upsetting. Shelters were being built. Most of the St Peter's children were evacuated to Wootton Bassett, a small country town in Wiltshire. Few of the residents of this quiet haven welcomed these little foreign cockneys into their homes. When families went to visit their children it didn't take them long to realise that the children were unhappy, unwanted and very homesick for the Quarter and the Italian way of life. Then, as nothing seemed to be happening (the period known as the phoney war gave people a false sense of security) they started to return to London. A temporary school was set up in St Peter's and for a short spell things seemed to be all right. Realisation hit home when a few of the young lads from the Hill who had been fighting with the British forces in France returned home with stories of the hell they had experienced during the evacuation from Dunkirk.

At 8 am on the day after Italy entered the war on the side of the Germans (15 May 1940), Raffaele and Duilio were picked up from the house in Warner Street by plain-clothes police. Lu had already left for work. Panic set in when news of the sinking of the Arandora Star broke. Thankfully, Raffaele was among the lucky ones who had been sent to the Isle of Man instead of Canada. Paola Maria did not see Raffaele for a year, until restrictions were lifted and wives and families were allowed to visit their menfolk at the internment camp.

In the absence of imported foods the Terroni delicatessen faltered, but in some miraculous way was kept going. Bombs rained down on the Italian Quarter night after night. One terrible night the industrial centre that was Clerkenwell, with its warehouses, offices and factories seemed to be going up in smoke. The next morning the Terroni family had just left the house when it suffered a direct hit. The bomb demolished No.34 leaving No.32 standing just long enough for the family, assisted by a friend, to recover most of the furniture. Strong-minded little Paola Maria took charge. The loss of their home for 27 years was a devastating blow to the Terroni family, but the consolation was that the family remained intact. Paola Maria with Lu, Pip and Luisa moved into a small house in Wren Street, near Gray's Inn Road. In 1942 Lu married his childhood sweetheart, Bruna Zanelli and had their honeymoon as a day in Richmond: Lu was now registered as an alien and was not allowed to go beyond 5 miles from his home. Like Alfonso Nastri (p 79) he had to sign in regularly at the police station in Gray's Inn Road.

St Peter's School photograph, 1923. Back row, 1st on left, Bruna Zanelli. Second row, 2nd from left, Elena Assirati. Front row, 3rd from left, Lu Terroni.

The newly-weds settled down in Wren Street with Paola Maria and it was here that their two daughters were born.

Luisa married Peter Di Giuseppe, a member of the family that had been known in the Quarter as barbers for many years. But young Peter studied accountancy and ended up as a partner in Ernst & Young. Peter's business was in Leather Lane until he retired in the 1980s. The couple had one son.

Pip, the youngest son of Raffaele and Caterina, married Peter's sister Carolina Di Giuseppe in 1944. Their eldest son Raffaele, who bears his grandfather's name, is a concert pianist, their other son John travels worldwide for Philips Petroleum, and their daughter Maria works with deaf children.

When Cavaliere Raffaele Terroni returned home from the internment camp in 1944 he was not allowed to go back to the family business but had to do work connected with the war effort. Lu continued to assist Roberto in the deli.

The war ended in 1945. What a joy it was to see the celebration of Our Lady of Mount Carmel return to the streets of Clerkenwell. Raffaele walked alongside Santa Lucia once again. With the war over and the pleasures of peacetime resumed, Bruna spent happy times with her father-in-law. Indulging his passion for picking mushrooms, they would leave the house early in the morning and go to secret places in Epping Forest where they searched for mushrooms (secret because one Italian never lets on to another exactly where the best *funghi* can be found). Raffaele would pick only *porcini*. He had a nose for seeking out the biggest and the best, and would stop and point to the spot with his umbrella, where, sure enough, would be a prize specimen. Raffaele was a good-natured family man; he loved children and during this period he was able to devote more time to his grandchildren.

The family moved to Highbury in 1949. Trade was picking up and rationing was tapering off. With the war years behind them Duilio and Raffaele joined Roberto in the shop where it was business as usual. In 1954 Bruna gave birth to a third daughter, Anna. When the baby was 8 months old, Paola was in Saviono visiting her daughter Rina. Raffaele was preparing to join her when he was taken ill and, after a very short illness, died. The family were devastated. He was only 65 years old.

Life went on, as it does, though Little Italy would never be the same. There were still many old residents left in the surrounding flats and in the little group of prefabs which had been built as temporary homes to replace the houses and shops in Little Bath Street. Joe Bacuzzi, the well-known, capped, English footballer, lived in one of these with his wife Phyllis and two young sons. Many of the former residents who had moved into the surrounding areas constantly returned to the Hill to meet in the Coach and Horses. On most evenings you would find both bars reverberating with the laughter of regulars such as Damso Molinari, Johnny Bergomini, Jimmy Falco, and the younger generation of men, as they teased their old pal Lou, the proprietor, and enjoyed playing popular Italian card games or darts. There was also plenty going on at St Peter's Church, where the Children of Mary and various other groups still met. The large tenements: Victoria Dwellings, Cavendish Mansions, Farringdon Buildings, Griffin Mansions and Corporation Buildings, were still inhabited by a mixture of Italians, Irish and Cockneys. Many of the younger married couples, second and third generation Italians, and Irish, lived on the Bourne Estate, a massive council block with a large entrance in Clerkenwell Road and bordering Leather Lane. On Sunday mornings after Mass old friends would go for a chat in Terroni's, which would be packed with ex-residents of the Hill all buying their wine, pastas, salamis, olives, Italian hams, cheeses etc.

After Roberto died in 1961 at the age of 76, Lu and Duilio carried on running the business, which, with the influx of a new generation of immigrants, was booming. Pasta was back in fashion and Italian food generally was in demand. Lu went on to follow in Raffaele's and Duilio's footsteps by taking on the job of Honorary Secretary of The Benevolent Society and, like his forebears, was honoured as Cavaliere.

Lu's daughters grew up in the house in Highbury. At 11 Paola went to St Aloysius Girls' Convent in Euston, whereas Stephanie, who was keen on sport, enjoyed her schooldays at William of York mixed comprehensive. Anna, the youngest, was still in primary school. Lu and Bruna were still living among friends from the old days, as a large number of Italians had settled in Highbury, in some ways a home from home.

One evening in 1963, when Paola was 18, she announced that she wanted to become a nun. Lu and Bruna at first thought it was a joke, but then strenuously opposed the idea. However, Paola persisted, joined the Order of the Faithful Companions of Jesus as a novitiate, spent two years at the Stella Maris Convent in

Terroni family

Paola Terroni (left) meeting Pope John Paul II with her Mother Superior

Broadstairs, then four years in Fribourg, Switzerland, and finally went to university there and graduated in French and geography. She returned to England and taught in Liverpool, Manchester and Birkenhead, eventually serving as headmistress at Gumley House Convent, Isleworth. In 1993 she was elected Superior General, head of the order.

Stephanie worked alongside her father Lu in the business until her marriage in 1973 to Carmine Carnevale, whose company manufactures many items such as Italian cheeses and, like the Terroni family, imports Italian produce. They have two sons and two daughters.

Anna went into banking and in due course married Emilio Di Silva, a Lloyds underwriter and director. They met at Stephanie's wedding and now have three sons. *Nonna* Paola Maria lived with Bruna and Lu all her life and attended every one of her grandchildren's weddings. She died in December 1979 aged 86.

The familiar shop in Clerkenwell Road finally left the hands of the Terroni family when Lu and Duilio retired in 1983, selling the business to the Anessa family.

Extracts from an article by Duilio Terroni entitled 'Mi ricordo' ('I remember')

"I remember the ice cream vendors, all from Southern Italy, who bought their ice from the local ice vendor, originally Fraulo & Perelli. They would boil the milk in their kitchens and then bring the cooled milk onto the pavements outside their homes. They proceeded to freeze it in zinc vats surrounded by ice, inside the wooden barrels. They would stir the mixture until it reached the right consistency, then with their neighbours' help load the vats onto adaptable barrows, decorated with pictures of Italian Royalty and sometimes English Royalty of the time. Then they proceeded on foot to various parts of London to sell their goods.

"In the days I grew up on the Hill, there was great poverty and shortage of work all round. The only option for Italian emigrants was to work on their own initiative as ice cream vendors, barbers, shoe repairers, porters, etc. The Hill was like a small Italian village, fully self-contained. It had its own butcher, grocers, shoe repairers, café, public house, fruiterer and even its own shoeshine boy, who would shine shoes for 2 old pence.

"On Sundays the junction of Warner Street, Bath Street and Eyre Street Hill was like a piazza and everybody, especially in the summer, would be out, passing the time outside the Italian Church, exactly as they still do today. Most families who could afford it prepared the roast, then took it to the baker on the corner to be cooked, since very few people owned cookers.

"Padre Antonio and Padre Crescitelli, the two Italian priests at that time, looked after their flock with great zeal and affection, always finding a word of encouragement and good cheer for those they met in the streets.

"St Peter's School was dedicated to teaching Italian to the children of the colony in the evenings. The teachers were all Italian and very devoted. One remembers most clearly: Maestro Ferrari, Maestro Persighetti, and Maestre Balestreri and Bisoni, who for many years assisted in the Italian evening classes to great effect.

"I remember the visit to London in 1914 of the Italian King and Queen [see also p 88]. Twelve coachloads of Italian children went to Grosvenor Square, to the Italian Embassy, to cheer their monarchs, who responded by making an appearance on the balcony of the Embassy.

"I remember the altar boys (40 in all) attending the High Mass every Sunday and in the evening at Vespers.

"I remember, at the end of the first World War, the memorable visit of the famous 'Bersaglieri', who had won a contest in London. They appeared that day in 'Little Italy,' demonstrating their well-known and well-loved fast military trot, to entertain their compatriots.

"I remember: the organ-grinders who were forced to push their organs around the West End streets to try to obtain some source of income.

"I remember: the street cleaners, who used hosepipes to wash the streets clean. We children would have great fun paddling in the water left behind. In those days we used to play cricket and football in the streets. St Peter's School had one of the best teams in Islington, and they won many shields.

"I remember: when, a fortnight before Christmas, the families prepared small altars and mangers with little statuettes of the Holy Family in their homes. Those who had altars were then visited by wandering minstrels. Two that I remember were Mr Voltrona and Mr Mancini, who went from house to house, singing carols and playing the flute and the violin. They were always followed by a bunch of kids from the Hill.

"I remember the first man to own a car in Back Hill. Guess who? The local bookmaker, and he would often give us kids a ride as a treat.

"I remember the wonderful weddings that took place in Little Italy. The bride and groom would leave the Church in a horse-drawn carriage and drive down Eyre Street Hill and up Bath Street, while all the Italian people would come out to wish them well, spraying them with flowers and confetti. When someone highly regarded died in Little Italy a very solemn funeral would take place and the colony would follow the cortège, sometimes led by a military band, all the way to the cemetery.

"I remember the first Italian Club being founded at 10 Laystall Street, where the plaque commemorating Giuseppe Mazzini can still be found. There is also a plaque in Hatton Garden where he used to live. Little Italy was also the home of great Italian industrialists such as Negretti and Zambra, Pastorelli and Casartelli."

Terroni family

Anita Maria Rosa Besagni, née Fassini

**The compiler of this book, Olive Besagni, tells the story
of her husband Bruno's mother, Anita Besagni.
Anita Maria Rosa Ferri left her homeland in 1919,
to live in the Italian Quarter with her parents and sisters.**

Ferri family

Anita Maria Rosa's parents, Maria Ferri and Pietro Fassini, were married in
Vernasca, Maria's home village, in the late 1800s. The Ferri family owned
a very small farm which nestled on the outskirts of Vernasca, in the province of
Piacenza. Maria had five sisters – Italina, Virginia, Adele and Anita – and four
brothers: Giuseppe who was in the army, Vittorio and Giacomo who helped to run
the farm, and Cesire who was the village postman.

Pietro Fassini's beginnings were something of a mystery; he seemed to be a
foundling, reared in an orphanage, and he had a half-brother whose surname was
Nanni. These two men were as alike as twins.

Maria and Pietro lived in a very small house close to her parents. Pietro
worked for a time in Lugagnano as a miner. He was a clever young man but he had
had no schooling, because the family who took him out of the foundling home,
though kind to him, had kept him working on their land from dawn till dusk. The
couple were very much in love: Pietro adored his wife and tried hard to improve
their lot. They were happy – he had a great sense of humour. Later four daughters
came along: Cesira, born 1900, Anita Maria Rosa in 1902, Rosa in 1909 and Elisa
in 1911. The family was were just about surviving with help from Maria's family.

In 1911 Italy declared war on Turkey in a bid to obtain Libya. Pietro
received papers calling him up. Knowing that he would be sent to Tripoli, that
army pay was a pittance, and that his family would be even worse off than before,
he decided to flee to Paris, where he heard there was a better chance of work. He
and Maria reluctantly left Vernasca, leaving the younger children in the care of 11-
year-old Cesira. Unbelievable behaviour as this seems to us today, desperate means
lead to desperate measures, and at least they knew that the nearby Ferri family
would ensure that the children would not starve.

In Paris there was no work; they lived Maria's earnings as a wet nurse for
more fortunate families. As a deserter Pietro could not return to Italy. Maria
returned alone to Vernasca and her children, while Pietro made his way through
Germany and Poland seeking work; she was not to set eyes on him for 7 years.

Vernasca, 1911-1918

Maria and the girls stayed on in the little house where money and food were sparse.
Maria's mother and sisters on the Ferri farm helped out as much as they could, but
these were tough times. Whenever the opportunity arose for the youngsters to earn

a lira or two, fruit picking, or doing other work in the surrounding countryside, they would go out into the fields and work all day for a pittance.

When Cesira was 14 she was taken to England by her Aunt Italina. There had been no sign or word in 3 years from Pietro, indeed no one was sure if he was alive or dead. As she waved her mother and sisters goodbye she wondered if she would ever see them again. The aunt and niece soon found work as waitresses in a café in London. Friends from home had helped them find a place to sleep in rooms in Clerkenwell, so that a few pennies were soon finding their way back to Cesira's mother and sisters.

Back in Vernasca Anita, now 13 years old, had grown into a vivacious, attractive girl. Full of life and energy, she responded with enthusiasm to any calls from the neighbouring farms during the harvest season. She would also work in the rice fields all day for a sack of rice, which she would then have to haul several miles to get it home. Even after a day's drudgery, standing for hours in water in the rice fields, she was always ready to entertain her aunts and cousins with her singing and dancing. She looked forward every day to letters from Cesira, though these were few as Italy was now in the throes of WW I.

Pietro Fassini, 1911-1918

After Pietro saw his wife off on the train he tried in vain to find work in Paris, then reluctantly left on a long journey through Germany, Poland and Scandinavia to St Petersburg. When he met other Italians making the same journey or on their way back home, he asked them to let his wife and children know he was alive and well. Because of his lack of schooling he was unable to read or write. Maria never received the messages. Pietro travelled on, doing various jobs, earning enough to feed himself. He gained a travelling companion, an Italian from the same region, and the two men eventually found work as field hands cutting grain on a Russian farm on the outskirts of St Petersburg. The farmer had taken a liking to Pietro and allowed the two men to sleep in his barn. They were earning a pittance, but at least they had food. The farmer eventually offered Pietro the job of managing his large warehouse where the grain was stored. He was given the keys and he would open up for the grain supplies to be delivered or collected and was responsible for locking up at night. With the small increase in his wage, he could afford to rent a room and also add a little more to his savings. There must have been days when he despaired of ever seeing his wife and children again.

By 1914 almost the whole of Europe was at war. By 1917 the Russian armies had to disengage in order to try to stem the Revolution, and the country was in chaos. One morning some soldiers ordered Pietro to open the warehouse. They entered and began to pull rifles out of the barrels of grain. Pietro, terrified, rushed to the farmer, handed him the keys and got out. In the weeks that followed Pietro witnessed horrific atrocities. One terrible day he saw some women digging a ditch at gunpoint, then the gunmen shot the women and kicked them into the grave they had just dug.

He knew then that he had to leave the country. On the way to the border he and his friend met other refugees making their escape, all in fear of their lives. They linked up with an Italian couple who, with their two youngest sons, were also fleeing. Their family name was Paradiso and they had been living in Russia for many years. Several of their older sons had been conscripted into the Russian Army. They had no idea where their sons were, or if they were dead or alive. They were hoping to get to England via Finland, and Pietro decided to travel with them.

The terrain was rough and the air unbelievably cold. The group, always cold and hungry, relied almost entirely on the generosity of surviving smallholders for scraps of food or milk for the children. Whilst travelling through Finland they met up with another Italian family, the young father from Northern Italy and the wife a Finnish girl. Their surname was Vellini and they had young children with them; their destination too was England. Pietro stayed with these two families, but his Italian friend decided to try to get back to his home, Piacenza, by travelling inland. Much as Pietro wanted to return home too, he wasn't sure how he stood with the Italian authorities over his failure to go and fight in Libya. He decided to trust his friend with the money that he had struggled to put by for his family during his years in exile. He handed his savings to his friend, instructing him to give Maria the money and let her know that he was still alive and on his way to England. He kept enough for his fare, and joined his newly-made friends.

England, Journey's End, 1918-1919

The Paradiso family, the Vellinis and Pietro continued on the last leg of the journey. They crossed the Baltic Sea, eventually disembarking in England, where life was returning to normality as the country celebrated the end of the Great War. Their destination was Victoria, where they were met by officials whose job it was to assist immigrants to a place of shelter. Whether through their advice or otherwise, their next stop was Clerkenwell, the Italian Quarter, where the other two families soon found lodgings. Pietro's one aim now was to get in touch with his family. He wished to return to Vernasca, but he had no passport. He was advised to go to the Italian consulate.

He was setting off for the consulate on foot through Soho when a million-to-one chance brought him face to face with his eldest daughter, Cesira. Seven years had passed since she had last seen him and Pietro was startled at first to find a pretty young lady throwing her arms round his neck and calling him "*Papa!*" She was now working as a waitress in an Italian café in Soho. She had only spotted her father when one of the waitresses, looking out of the window of the café, had pointed out this strange-looking man in Russian style clothing and wearing a fur Cossack hat. "What are you doing here?" she asked. "I'm going to the consulate to get a passport. I must get home to Vernasca to your mother and your sisters. How are they? Is everything all right with them? And what are you doing here?" As you can imagine, many tears were shed. She took her father to the room in Leicester

Place, a little mews off Little Saffron Hill, where she had been painstakingly building up a home in preparation for her mother and sisters, who were already going through the formalities in Italy necessary for them to emigrate. Cesira had been in England for four years, had a steady job and could provide them with a home. All Pietro had to do was wait.

Cesira had furnished the room in Leicester Place very nicely with all the necessities available in those austere times. The mere fact that there was an outside toilet, albeit shared with several other families, was a revelation. Pietro was so happy; the situation he found himself in now was the best that he'd ever known. He had friends nearby, the Paradiso family in rooms just along the street in Little Saffron Hill and the Vellini family settled in the heart of the hill, just across Warner Street. The three families retained their friendship for many years.

Anita Maria Rosa Besagni née Fassini

The Fassini family reunited at last

Back in Vernasca Maria with her three remaining daughters waited patiently for the documents to be completed that would allow them to come to England. (I found a visa-like card that was part of the documentation necessary to enable my mother-in-law Anita Fassini, to travel as an emigrant. It was entitled *Certificato Di Miserabilità*, meaning that the emigrant was living in a state of abject poverty. When we see a document of this nature it brings home to us why so many people had no choice other than to pack up and leave their lovely homeland and all their friends and relations there.)

Cesira Fassini, who recognised her father after his 7 years of wandering

It must have been an emotional reunion when Maria and her daughters finally arrived in the Italian Quarter. I wonder if Anita felt excitement or dismay as she viewed the cobbled streets and alleyways, the eerie shadows cast by the gas-lit street lamps and experienced the noise, the rattle of trams and the general cacophony of sound that was London in those days. The Hill dwellers would be milling about, there would be groups standing around on street corners, children playing in the gloom around the gas lamps, the plaintive sounds of *"Santa Lucia,"* from one of the many street organs in the area, intermingled with the cries of the chestnut vendor and the clip-clopping of the horses' hooves on the cobbled streets as they pulled the ice carts bearing huge blocks of ice to be left outside the shops and restaurants. When the family finally entered Leicester Place, all the residents were out trying to get a look at the newcomers.

In the rooms in No.4 where they were together again after so many years apart, there were new white net curtains at the windows, a stove, china and cutlery, furniture and all the things necessary to make a home. It did not matter that you had to go down into the communal scullery in the basement for your water or that the toilet was in the yard. Pietro now had a job too, so there was plenty of food on the table. Those two rooms in Leicester Place must have seemed like Buckingham Palace to the newcomers.

So what did the future hold in store for Anita? She was 18 years old, attractive, fit and strong. She soon got a job with Cesira, who was by now a waitress in Bertorelli's restaurant in Charlotte Street. Life must have seemed very rosy, and a wage at the end of the week! Naturally most of the money went to her mother, Maria, but with the rest she was able to buy nice clothes, shoes and to treat her little sisters now and again.

Pietro Fassini (Studio portrait)

Their first Christmas in England was spent with Aunt Italina who lived in Bell Street, off Edgware Road, where, as you can imagine, they savoured many new delights: an abundance of food and wine, English chocolate and toys and fruit for the little ones. Imagine how Pietro must have felt as he feasted his eyes on his wife and children, the long, lonely years spent alone in Russia fast receding into the background. The baby of the family, 8-year-old Elisa, was so taken with the taste of chocolate she had enjoyed on Christmas Day that the following day she thought that she would like some more.

So she set off alone to find her Auntie Italina's home. Her idea was to follow the tramlines until she reached her auntie's home, but she soon lost her bearings. Fortunately she was spotted by one of the priests from the Italian Church who found her sitting on a doorstep, crying. They were unable to communicate very well as the priest could not understand her dialect which was, of course, the only Italian that the child knew. He did not know the Fassini family as they had just moved into the area, so he took her to the police station. Elisa recalled sitting on the counter in the station and seeing a lady with only one eye whom she remembered from the boat coming to England. The woman recognised Elisa and mercifully knew where the family lived. Cesira and Anita rushed to the station to pick her up. The panic when the Fassinis realised that Elisa was missing is not hard to imagine.

The family had settled into their new home. Pietro now had a permanent smile on his face. Rosa and Elisa attended St Peter's Italian School immediately across from Leicester Place. None knew better than Pietro how important education was: he had suffered woefully on account of his illiteracy. There were plenty of friends and relatives nearby and Maria was never lonely. Anita and Cesira attended Italian evening classes when the long hours they worked permitted. And dances were held in the rooms above the church.

Living in the rooms above them in the house in Leicester Place were a family from Teruzzi which lies just above Morfasso, not very far from Vernasca; they were Margherita and Giuseppe Besagni with their daughter Maria and two sons, Antonio (Tony) and Giovanni (Johnny). The boys had served in the Italian Army throughout the 1914-1918 war.

The older boy, Tony, had got married in Italy and lived with his young wife and their three young children on the top floor of the house. The younger son, Giovanni (Johnny), was still serving in the Italian Army. There were several other families at that address during this period but we will concentrate on those we have mentioned.

Anita Maria Rosa Besagni née Fassini

Giovanni and Antonio Besagni during World War I

Pietro had a regular job at the Connaught Rooms, a large banqueting hall in Holborn, albeit a fairly humble job cleaning the silver, but it was regular and it provided a steady income. He was a jocular man who got on well with his fellow workers. He spent many an evening playing *bocce* with his Italian friends on a pitch that had been set up next to the Gunmakers' Arms in Eyre Street Hill. *Bocce* (bowls) was very popular in Italy, and it goes without saying that quite a few glasses of wine would be consumed in the course of the game.

Pietro adored his wife and daughters and the home would ring with their laughter. Of course he kept a strict eye on the two older girls, and any young man looking in their direction was sent packing. Sometimes he was a particularly happy man when he returned from Dondi's or the Coach and Horses with a song on his lips and a new friend in tow. At these times his little Maria would chide him in no uncertain terms, though he usually ended up making her laugh, whereupon all would be forgiven.

Cesira was the first to get married, to Guglielmo Teagno who was head wine waiter in a Soho restaurant. They set up home in a top-floor flat in Highbury, where they remained for many years. In time Cesira gave birth to two children, Renato and Rosina.

Anita in the meantime had spread her wings a little further. Unbeknown to her parents, one evening she had gone to a dancehall in Clerkenwell Green, just a step away from 'the Hill', but out of bounds to daughters of Italian families. She was noticed by a handsome young Italian. He invited her to dance and she was instantly smitten. By an extraordinary coincidence he turned out to be the younger son of the Besagni family, Giovanni (Johnny), recently demobbed from the Italian Army where he had been finishing his service. He was a corporal and in 1918 had been awarded *la Croce Merito di Guerra*. He had recently come to England to join his parents in the room above the Fassinis. It was not long before the young couple were married at St Peter's Italian Church, on 14 May 1922.

Anita and Johnny

They opened a small café in King's Cross Road. Like many of their friends, catering was second nature to them. At first things went well, but when the babies started arriving – Renaldo in 1923, Rita in 1924, and Bruno in 1925, they were unable to continue with the café so they moved back to Clerkenwell, to a self-contained flat in Victoria Dwellings, just around the corner from her mother, who was then able to help with the babies. No.57 consisted of two rooms on the ground floor, which was handy as there were now three little ones, and a fourth was imminent. They were surrounded by numbers of friends with big families, like themselves from Piacenza, and there was an English family called Snow with ten children living in the basement. Anita was popular, always ready to help her neighbours when she could. She was never lonely, even though Johnny worked very long days for the Ragusa Asphalt Company. It was hard work but the wages were good. He had to travel a lot and most of his workmates were Italian.

In 1926, 4-year-old Renaldo, a beautiful child with dark curly hair and big brown eyes, died from pneumonia. The loss of a toddler or an infant was common enough at that time; the effect on the mothers must always have been traumatic, but they had to carry on for the sake of their other children. The years that followed were very hard for Anita. She kept her children spotlessly clean, the rooms neat and tidy, and she was always scrubbing and cooking. She spent most of her days *incinta* (pregnant), so the close proximity of her mother was a great help. Maria spent most of her time with Anita and the children. The little ones adored their grandparents and they loved to go down to Leicester Place where they would always find a sweet in an apron pocket or a drawer.

Johnny was rarely home. His work took him away for days at a time and even when the job was nearer home, he would come home so tired that, once he had had a meal he would go to the pub, and sit on a bar stool chatting to his old friend the landlord, Lou Resteghini. He needed to escape the crowded flat, away from crying babies and noisy children, returning only when they were all tucked up in bed.

One morning little Rita was run over by a cyclist, and what at first seemed only a minor injury developed into osteomyelitis, which plagued her for the rest of her days. She lived much of her early life in Carshalton Children's Hospital, where

Anita Besagni and Angelina (Antonio's wife) visiting Lidia and Rita in Carshalton

she spent months at a time as an inpatient. Then Lidia developed rickets and had to wear leg braces, so she also spent weeks in the same hospital. Either Anita or Johnny visited one or both of them every weekend for at least 3 years. Despite their many trials, Anita's old friends and neighbours say how hospitable and kind she was and how she always had time and sympathy for other people's problems.

In 1938 there were nine surviving children, and Anita's life was considerably easier: the older girls helped with the babies and the housework and there was always someone to run errands. In spite of all the ups and downs, Anita had progressed: she had learnt to read English by perusing the daily newspapers and she made the children's clothes. She was an excellent cook and could make a dinner stretch further than anyone I had ever known. If the family were having dinner and a visitor or even the children's friends called, another chair would be put at the table, and the visitor would be pressed to "*mangia - mangia*" (eat – eat!).

The highlight of their year was the annual procession of Our Lady of Mount Carmel. All their children walked in the procession as soon as they were old enough, and Anita made all their costumes, until Rita, who was an excellent dressmaker, took over from her mother.

Bruno was the only one of the children who ever had a holiday at the seaside. Being the oldest boy he was taken on several holidays by his two young aunts, Rosa and Elisa Fassini. The two girls had blossomed into beauties and whenever they went on holiday, usually to Clacton-on-Sea, their father Pietro would allow them out only with a chaperone. Bruno, who was only 8 years old, always had a wonderful week being indulged with any amount of ice cream and Tizer (the leading fizzy drink of the day), swimming and rides at the funfairs – he was in heaven. When they returned home he would be bribed by his *Nonno* Pietro to tell who they had been with and what they had been up to. He would then be bribed by his aunts not to tell.

For Anita, a day at the seaside would have been an impossible dream. But she had her Johnny and her children, and she made the best of it. The advent of WW II in 1939 brought really bad times. The older children remained at home, Rita working as a seamstress; 14-year-old Bruno was about to start his first job with an optical company. Lidia, in her last year at school, was in Italy on a holiday with the *Ballila* (Italian Scouts and Guides). Pino, Olga, Ines and Remo were sent with the rest of their school to Wootton Bassett. Anita stayed in London with her two youngest, Maria and Dorina. The first year of the war passed. Lidia, still in Italy, had left the main party to stay with her mother's relatives in Vernasca but, as the situation worsened, she was unsure what to do. She was only 13 and when it began to look as if Italy was going to join in the war, she wanted to get home. She found a woman in the village who was coming back to London and persuaded her to bring her back.

In London things were quiet. There were no bombs in that first year but things were not going so well for Ines and Olga in the country. The little girls were unhappy and being ill treated. They had had two bad billets in succession so Johnny went down to the village, disliked what he saw, and brought them back to Clerkenwell and Mamma.

Then it all happened, the worst possible news for the Italians. Italy had joined Hitler and his Nazis. Immigrant Italian men began to be interned. They came for Johnny and he packed his case with his wife and children in tears around him. But then, for some reason, after investigation he was sent home. But he lost his job with the asphalt company, the job he loved and where he had made a name for himself. All those years of work counted for nothing. Then Pietro was sacked from his job in the Connaught Rooms, where he had worked ever since he arrived in England.

In the midst of all the sadness, Anita was *incinta* again, and the bombing had now started in earnest. Anita took Ines and Olga to Wales where her mother Maria and sister Elisa were staying in a house belonging to a friend. She left the girls there and returned to London to be with Johnny, but by this time the bombing was so bad that, with Maria a toddler and Dorina a baby, she had to flee to the country yet again. Now it was to Wootton Bassett, where at least she would be near Remo and Pino, who had stayed there in a decent billet with a

Mrs Pincot who had become a family friend.

Anita had been allocated a small cottage outside the village, very primitive, but she did her best to make it a home for herself and the girls. It was in this cottage that the youngest of her children was born, Giovanni, known later as Johnny, like his father. Husband Johnny went to work as a cook for his sister Maria (Oddi) who had a café in Hammersmith. He put up with it, but he never really recovered from the change. He did not like being indoors in a windowless basement instead of outdoors working in the asphalt trade.

Quite early in the war, when the bombing was at its height, the family was dealt another devastating blow. Pietro (*Nonno*), terrified of the air raids, spent his nights sleeping in Chancery Lane underground station. One morning, returning home on the bus with a couple of friends and sitting next to his neighbour, Mrs Belli, he put his head on her shoulder. She thought he was larking about, but when she tried to move him, she realised he was dead.

After the turmoil of the war years, the Besagni family's finances began to improve. Bruno, Rita, Lidia and Pino had jobs. Johnny (*Papa*) had continued working in his sister's café in Hammersmith. When the children returned from being evacuated, the flat at No.57 was overcrowded, but with the easing of the financial situation they were able to rent another flat in the same block, a two-roomed flat with a kitchen, running water and an inside toilet. Three of the boys shared one bedroom and the four older girls had the other. Little Maria, now 8 years old, was sleeping with her *Nonna* Maria in Leicester Place. She awoke one night to find that her *Nonna* had not come to bed. She found her sitting in the armchair and could not rouse her, so she called a neighbour and ran up the road to call her parents. *Nonna* Maria had slipped away as she dozed. Young Maria remembers running as fast as she could along the poorly lit road of Little Saffron Hill: only a couple of minutes but to the little girl it seemed more like a mile. Poor Anita, her beloved mother! She mourned for a long time; they had been through so much together.

The war had also had an effect on Lidia. She was 18 years old when American G.I.s first appeared in London. Many of these young soldiers were Italian Americans and when they realised that there were several young girls in the area who were also of Italian extraction, they would make themselves known by calling out "*Eh! Paesana.*" The girls would realise that these American boys were, like themselves, emigrants from Italy. Lidia brought several of these young men home and Anita would give them a plate of pasta and make them feel at home. When the war was over Lidia would settle for nothing less than to go to America. Her father, Johnny, was against the idea but Anita, who understood her daughter's desire to better herself, supported her, so off she went to the USA.

The sad days were not over for Anita. Her beloved Johnny had been unwell and after a short while it was found that he was suffering from throat cancer. He died leaving a devastated Anita a widow, still in her early 40s. But Anita's resilience was amazing. Four of her daughters followed Lidia to the

Anita Maria Rosa Besagni née Fassini

States, where in time they all married Americans.

The first to return home for a holiday was Lidia. Nine years had elapsed when she came home on the Queen Mary with three of her children (Raymond aged 9, Alfred 7, and Linda 5). Imagine the excitement created by this visit. The tears, of happiness this time, as the family waited anxiously on the platform at Victoria Station, the joy as she came into view with her three children. Anita was overcome. Lidia had such vitality and she had been sadly missed. Anita was never to wait so long again without seeing her daughters. As the family in England was now grown up, she started travelling back and forth to the States as if it was Brighton, and on each visit being treated like a queen.

Bruno has never forgotten the first time he took her to the ship to go to America. Anita had always been sociable and she was soon chatting to her cabin-mate. He waved goodbye to his *Mamma* Anita, soberly dressed and looking every bit the Italian mother. When she returned after her 6-month visit, Bruno and his brothers went to meet her at Victoria. They were met by a smart young woman with a modern hairstyle, red shoes, red hat and dark pink nail varnish, looking fantastic. Her life changed dramatically. She flew back and forth to Connecticut frequently and her daughters could not get enough of her. There were also trips to Vernasca, to visit her relatives there.

Always a wonderful mother and *Nonna* to her children and grandchildren in London, her last years living with her daughter Olga at Highgate were very happy. They lived in a large house with Olga's two sons, John and Michael. Olga was the only daughter to stay in London, very happily married to Albert Cavalli, whose father also lived with them. The girls from America were also now travelling back and forth, and her sons with their wives were constant visitors to the house in Highgate. She loved a party, and no invitation was ever turned down. Returning from a party one night, she said to Olga, "I'm very tired," sat down on a chair and left us. What a sad day for her children and her family, but what a life! And what lovely memories she left behind.

Avella and Monti family: the four Carmelas

Gaetano & Carmela: the late 1880s

Angelo Avella outside Gaetano's shop, 1914

Bidding their little daughter Carmela (No.2) what must have been a traumatic farewell and leaving her in the care of their families, who lived in the little town of Avellino, near Naples, Gaetano and Carmela (No.1) (née Vecchione) Avella, a young couple searching for a better life, made their way to England. The young couple settled in the Italian Quarter, and being of an entrepreneurial nature they soon started up a small business at Nos.4-4a Eyre Street Hill, in the heart of the Quarter. Gaetano was a baker, and baked the bread and cakes for the shop. In the basement they made their own wine from grapes delivered from Covent Garden. Everything sold in their shop was made on the premises, including their own Italian sausages, *salami*, and *crabette*, a meat – possibly goat, as they kept two nanny-goats in the back yard to provide goat's cheese and milk. So the Avellas were soon providing most things that the Italian housewife would require. However, with the arrival of a couple of bears in a yard next to their premises, they moved shop and family up the road to No.19!

Once they were settled in London they sent for their only daughter Carmela (No.2). Angelo (Charlie) was born in 1888, then Michele (Micky), followed by Giovanni, Dominic and finally Gaetano (Peche); six children, a relatively small family by the standards of the era. Even so, how hard Carmela (No.1) must have worked, with such limited facilities, raising a family, not only running a business but making most of the produce they sold, ice cream soon being added to the other comestibles. Avella's provision shop at 19 Eyre St Hill was as familiar to Hill residents as the church and the school. It was always filled to capacity: *salamis* and *baccala* hung from the ceiling, floor space being taken up with barrels of anchovies, olives and lubeans, big metal milk churns, and large old-fashioned drawers filled with various kinds of pasta, just about everything that an Italian family could require. Gaetano (Peche) eventually married Tarqinia (Queenie) Terroni (p 102), daughter of Duilio Terroni, a member of the well-known Terroni family of the delicatessen in Clerkenwell Road. They had three children, Peter, John and Maria. As a relatively young man, Peche became a familiar face in British films. Apparently one day he was walking along High Holborn when he was approached by a man who asked him if he would like to be in films. Peche, thinking it was a wind-up (as he was no Robert Taylor), told the man in no uncertain terms to "F... off". The man finally convinced him that he was serious and that they were looking

Carmela No.4 aged 16

for strong young men to take the part of gladiators in a new film, *Cleopatra*. Peche went along with it, and thereafter he was known as Peter Avella, seen on the screen in many other British films. He used to tell the story that, while he was being made up for his part as an extra in the making of *Oliver!* he was told "I don't know why they didn't cast you as Fagin – with your features you wouldn't have had to be made up, you're a natural".

The Avella children all grew up in Little Italy. Carmela (No.2), being the eldest and the only daughter, helped her Mamma to look after her young brothers and also helped in the shop; a common lot for daughters of Italian parents, whereas the boys were usually waited on by mother and sisters. Carmela (No.2) had a pretty hard life.

In 1927 she married Carlo Monti-Colombo, a fellow Southerner and a floor layer. The Avellas gave their daughter a huge wedding – they were already pretty well off. The young couple also prospered and eventually built up a very successful business, the well-known restaurant Carlo's, in Theobalds Road, a popular meeting place for young Italians.

Their only daughter, also named Carmela (No.4) after her mother and grandmother, was a beautiful child. She was followed by two boys, Antonio (Tony), and Carlo. Carmela (No.2) adored her children, and her sons loved their sister. As she was growing up and the young lads in the quarter were beginning to pay her attention, Tony and Carlo would send them packing. Sadly, young Carmela was showing signs of a debilitating illness, she was sent away to the Convent of the Immaculate Conception in Hampstead with her young cousin, Carmela (No.3) (see a little later), to keep her company and stop her from being lonely. The nuns made every effort to cure her, but in spite of all the efforts of doctors, the hospital and the many prayers of the community, the lovely young girl died at the early age of 18.

Sixteen-year-old Angelo (Charlie) can be seen in the photo (p 125) taken outside the family shop in Eyre Street Hill. His father Gaetano's skill in bread making is evidenced by the huge loaves visible in the shop window. Two years later

126

he was unfortunate enough to go to Italy to visit relatives in Avellino. WW I was still going on and, naturally, he was picked up by the Italian authorities and made to join the Italian Army, where he was put to work as an interpreter for two years. When the war ended he returned home and worked for several asphalt and terrazzo companies as an assessor and estimator. He was a Lodge member of the Italian Freemasons and in this capacity was able to assist Italian immigrants coming into the country by helping them to find work and a place to live within the community.

His mother, old Carmela (No.1), was something of a martinet, particularly where her children were concerned. When Angelo (Charlie), her second son, became enamoured of a young English girl, Mary Perrin, she did everything in her power to stop the marriage, but in the end love won through: Charlie married his English sweetheart and the couple were blessed with four children: Charlie (Bobos), Carmela (No.3), Anthony (Tony), and finally Gaetano (Dog). Dog came by this nickname because he appeared at school every day with a copy of a dog-racing paper. Giovanni (Johnny) was the musician of the family. He played several instruments, the violin being his forte. Johnny formed an orchestra, and changed his name to Raymon. The orchestra was billed as "Raymon Avella and his Famous International Symphonic Orchestra." It was a large orchestra consisting of 35 instrumentalists, and they played at many famous venues, for instance the Prince of Wales Theatre, the London Palladium, the Winter Garden in Berlin and on Radio Roma and Radio Luxembourg among others. Quite late in life he married a German girl named Anne.

Michaele (Micky), at the age of 18, went for a holiday to visit his father's brother in the USA, where he met and married his cousin, Olympia. They had two sons, Michael and Tony. Micky never returned to England, but his sister Carmela (No.2) and brothers made the long journey across the Atlantic by ship (planes would have been out of the question in those days) to visit him. The couple ran a successful business in Brooklyn and had a house on Long Island. Judging by the car in the photograph they were doing all right!

Dominic was a mosaic worker. He was conscripted into the British Army during WW II. On his return, with his wife Lena, he ran a café in Cross Street, Leather Lane. Lena was an excellent cook and always had a large saucepan of *pasta e fagioli* on the stove and, in neighbourly fashion, a plate of the same would be offered to any friends – and they were many – who happened by.

In the 1930s Sunday dinner at No.19 Eyre Street Hill was an enormous affair. All the Avella family and their offspring, friends and relatives would gather for one of Carmella (No.1)'s feasts. A massive table filled the room, with just enough space to seat everyone. The inevitable large plates of pasta were followed by massive main courses of steaks, sometimes goat's meat, plenty of salad and an abundance of wine and fresh fruit. Finally, handfuls of nuts would be thrown onto the table, amongst which would be pumpkin seeds, also known as 'take your time,' so called because of the length of time it took to get to the nut, but it was worth the effort once the delicacy was revealed. Quite often Father Kennedy from the

Italian Church would come and join the family for the repast.

After the meal the men would play cards, and on warm sunny days the women would sit outside the shop gossiping and watching the children playing in the street. The two young Carmelas played with the Aguda children, the Falcos, the Ricordis and the girl Cemini at whips and tops, hoops, hide-and-seek and ball games. The mothers did not have to watch the children when they played in streets of the quarter; they were safe, as everyone looked out for every child in the vicinity of the Hill. Carmela (No.3) always looked after her young cousin, Carmela (No.4) on account of her failing health (p 126).

When Carmela (No.3) was old enough to go dancing, her brothers always kept an eye on any young worthies who might be hovering, but one night at Holborn Hall she met a young man of the kind Italians call '*mesa mes*,' meaning half and half, in other words his mother was Italian (Filumena, a member of the Fiori family of Farringdon Road) and his father English. His name was Owen Pointing; he was a good friend of her brother Tony. Carmela and Owen were wonderful jivers, and could be seen every weekend at Holborn Hall happily jiving the night away. They actually won a contest and were offered a tour, which they declined. In 1952 Owen and Carmela were married and had two sons, Anthony and Michael.

Owen was an ambitious young man and tried his hand at everything, statue-making and plumbing among other trades, but was always dissatisfied. Then he took quite an unusual step. He was inspired to take a chance and applied for a low-grade job in the offices of a marine insurance company. Having landed the job, he applied for every promotion that came up and by sheer determination and with Carmela's encouragement, in no time became a member of the board and eventually a partner in the firm. The couple still live close to the Italian quarter on the Lloyd Baker Estate, but spend weekends at their beautiful thatched cottage in Sybil Headingham, a small village in Essex. Carmela never wants to leave the area so near to their roots. She is an excellent cook and they still keep up the Italian way of life, in the kitchen anyway, with *pasta e fagioli* often on the menu.

Anna Nataro
(Nanella, a child of the quarter)

Pasquale Nataro was born in Peckham in 1895. His parents, Aniello Nataro and his wife Anna, née Esposito, had earlier emigrated to London from the little town of Saviano in Southern Italy. When Pasquale was 2 years old, his young mother, Anna, became terminally ill and they returned to their native Saviano. After his mother died Pasquale remained in Saviano, where he was cared for by relatives. In 1922 he married Filumena Tufano, a local girl, and in 1923 Filumena gave birth to a baby girl, Anna (Nanella). Shortly after the baby's birth Pasquale bade his wife and child a sad goodbye and set off for England in search of work.

In London he found lodgings over a provisions shop in Baker's Row, and a job as a tinsmith. When Nanella was 18 months old, Pasquale sent for them. They soon found quarters on the top floor of a house in Leicester Place, where they lived above the Satori family. By now Pasquale had found a better job as a parquet floor layer with the Vecchione family's "Vigas" Company. Nanella looks back on her childhood days in Leicester Place as a good time in her life. She said: "In spite of the conditions that prevailed, they were very happy times". Her little sister, Lena, was born in 1926, soon followed in 1927 by baby Aniello. The birth of the first son was a source of great joy for Pasquale; for a Neapolitan man it is important to beget a boy so he can give the baby the name of his father, but at the age of 18 months baby Aniello was taken ill, and died before the doctor, summoned at 10 a.m., arrived in the evening. Filumena was so enraged with the doctor that she chased him downstairs, brandishing her broom. Nanella has crystal-clear memories of that very sad time. The baby was laid out in one of the rooms of their home: "To me as a child, it looked like a stage, with big candles at each end (my mother must have borrowed them from the church). He was a beautiful child with thick curly hair, dressed in a little white suit, with his hands clasped across his chest".

However, they were fortunate because in 1930 Filumena gave birth to a second son who naturally was also named Aniello; and two years later another daughter, Teresa.

Nanella remembers playing with her school friends Ines Birry and Rina Ricorda'. When she started school, she could not speak a word of English, but neither could many of her friends. The parents had enough trouble understanding the many different dialects of the Italian language in the small area of Little Italy! The school playground was a little yard adjacent to a garden behind the nuns' house, where on sunny days the nuns would hang out their washing. The girls spent their playtime peeping over the wall at the nuns' long underwear pegged on the line, trying to guess which pair belonged to which of the sisters.

Pasquale worked hard, often away from home, but there was always plenty of food on the table in the Nataro home. After Teresa's birth the flat got rather crowded, so the family moved to Lloyd Baker Street, off King's Cross Road, where several other Italian families had settled. So Bruno, Nanella's youngest brother, was the only member of the family to be born outside the Quarter.

The following years passed uneventfully. At the start of WW II Filumena and the children were evacuated to a small village in Suffolk. They were lucky to be billeted in a small cottage to themselves, where they spent the whole of the war. When they finally returned to Lloyd Baker Street, Nanella was in her late teens. She was allowed to go to dances only if accompanied by her brothers, sisters or cousins. Pasquale was a typical Italian father; he kept a strict eye on his daughters and they were never allowed to stay out late. One night in January 1951, at the 'Notre Dame' where many young Italians gathered to dance, she met a young Northern Italian boy, Remo Corradi. They were mutually attracted, but she didn't dare mention him to her father: his attitude was that if they brought a young man into the house they either married him or he was out.

On 14 February a Valentine card arrived at her home. When she returned from work, her father said: "There's a letter for you on the mantelpiece. It looks to me like Italian handwriting. Open it." She told him, "It's from a young man I've been dancing with at the club". She had a feeling that he already knew that she had met someone.

"Then he asked me about the boy's family. He could find no fault with Remo, who had a good job as a steward in First class on the Mauritania. He used to bring home presents from America – nylon stockings, a great luxury then – but Pasquale had taught his girls never to accept presents from young men and I was always afraid he would find out." Later, when her father met Remo, he took to him. Pasquale was introduced to the Corradis, who came from Monastero (Piacenza). The two families got on well. Nanella married Remo on 2 June 1952 and in 1954 a baby son, Renato, arrived. By now Remo was no longer travelling the world. He had a good position as a wine waiter at Simpson's in Piccadilly.

Pulisciano–Magrino family

Vince, a great character

When Vincent Magrino died in 2005 we lost a phenomenal array of memories and knowledge he had acquired of life as it was in the Italian colony. Vince was born in 1937, in the decade that was to see the end of the Italian Quarter. He had an incredible memory for faces and places and was always fascinated by Hollywood and the film stars and songs of the period. He had collected records, discs and tapes from the old days, and he was a mine of information. His phone was constantly ringing with friends and others checking on dates and melodies from the 1920s to the present day.

Vincent's friends – and he had many – contained a good number of well-known TV personalities. A visit to Vince's flat was never boring; before his mother died, the afternoon would be enlivened by exchanges of vivid expletives, in English and Italian, between the two of them, but they loved one another dearly and when she died he was bereft. Fortunately, one of his mother's sisters, Carmela, lived nearby, and when her health was failing Vince visited her daily and looked after her for the rest of her days. Vince was a real character, loved by his friends and family.

Here is the story of Vincent's mother's family, the Puliscianos, who lived in the heart of the Hill for many years. With Procession Sunday looming, I went to see Vince, knowing that he still kept open house on that day. He made ready for the day, as his mother and grandmother did before him, by preparing food and wine and sorting out just the right music, ready for the influx of people. Once the procession had passed and the walk around the *Sagra* (fête), greeting friends and relatives amongst the milling throng, was over, Vince hurried home and the party began. In the next few hours, dozens of friends and relatives would meet with cordiality and affection at the house in Phoenix Place, Mount Pleasant, a few minutes from the Hill. The conversation would have been largely about the old days 'down the Hill' and there were always friends of old standing there, however famous TV personalities they might be. Vince felt he had never left the Quarter. His knowledge about the life and times of 'the Hill' was backed up by a wonderful photograph collection of family, relatives and friends.

In 1895, Vince's grandparents, Maria and Vincenzo Pulisciano, made the journey to England from the small village of Senerchia (Avellino), Southern Italy. (Senerchia was one of the villages destroyed by the 1979 earthquake.) The couple came with their 7-year-old son Danano, who in his adult years in the 1920s and 1930s was well known down the Hill as 'Johnny the Barber'. Luckier than some other immigrants at that time, they had an address to go to, for one of their cousins, Carolina Tremarco, had preceded them. Vince had a document from that time which describes the Tremarco family's occupation as travelling musicians – "probably organ-grinders", Vince would say.

The Pulisciano family were soon in business. They set up a barber's shop in Warner Street and the business, like the family, thrived and increased. Gerardo was born in 1899, Carmela in 1901, Rosa in 1903, and finally Emma in 1904. Their father made a good living and, judging by the photographs, the children were well fed and well clothed.

Maria Pulisciano with daughters Carmela (the taller of the two standing), Rosa (later Magrino, Vince's mother), Emma (seated), and Little Giovanni. Procession Sunday 1912

In 1918 *Nonno* Vincenzo purchased the business and premises of a larger barber's shop at No.19 Great Bath Street. Vince showed me the original handwritten agreement or bill of sale. The price for the premises, fittings and stock included, was £15. A £2 deposit clinched the deal. The owner of the shop was Salvatore Fama. Salvatore was a tenor. After he sold the business he turned professional, making several recordings, and the Pulisciano family still have a record of him singing *Santa Lucia*.

The shop in Great Bath Street was to be the family home for many years. The rooms above the shop were let to lodgers, relatives and other immigrants. Pulisciano's *Barbiere Italiano* at No.19 Bath Street is remembered by all the families living in the Quarter. The Puliscianos were a lively, hospitable family. Several of them were drawn to acting, mainly in the musical field. The lovely photograph taken on Procession Sunday 1912 is of the three Pulisciano girls; the taller of the two standing is Carmela, standing next to her is Vince's mother Rosa, and the seated girl is Emma.

One of the lodgers, a cousin from Avellino named Adamo Magrino, set his cap at the young Rosa and the couple were married in 1923. The studio photograph of Rosa and Adamo, Vince's parents, was taken in 1928. The photo of the Procession in 1936 shows Bath Street and in the background the Pulisciano barber's shop can be seen, *Barbiere Italian* written on the glass.

Rosa and Adamo remained childless for 14 years, then in 1937 their son Vincenzo (Vince) was born in University College Hospital. During this period the authorities began moving the families out of the Quarter, the beginning of the end for Little Italy. When Vince was 2 the family moved into improved living conditions in Phoenix Place, Mount Pleasant.

Vince had always wanted to walk in the Procession, but because of WW II, six years passed before there could be another Procession Sunday. So Vince was 10 years old before his time came, in 1947. The young boy in front of the Altar Servers is Vincent Magrino, who died at 73 in 2005.

Also taking part in the same Procession were Giovanni and Maria Besagni (see p 123), dressed as a priest and a nun.

Vince Magrino, aged 10, in the first Procession after WW II (1947)

Giovanni and Maria Besagni dressed as priest and nun in the 1947 Procession.

133

Pino Maestri – the scribe

**He sowed the seed of interest
in the history of "Il Quartiere"
in the Backhill magazine**

"**M**y parents, Luigi Maestri and Rosina Domini, came to London just before the turn of the century. They were married in St Peter's Italian Church. Their first home was No.21 Eyre Street Hill, in the heart of the Italian Quarter. They had five children, the eldest Romeo, then Giulietta, myself (Pino), Elena, and Mario.

"Sadly, Giulietta caught diphtheria and died while still a child. My earliest recollection is sitting at the kerbside, crying as I watched the horse-drawn hearse carrying my sister's small coffin past our house.

"Our home was, to say the least, a very busy house. My parents let out some of the rooms to lodgers, most of whom, when they arrived in Clerkenwell, would be told: "Go to Rosina's," and they would stay with us for a short time until they found a place to settle. In our kitchen there were two tables: one for the family and one for the lodgers.

"It was quite common for the family to sell wine, unlicensed of course. For instance you could come to our place and order a glass of wine and sometimes there would be dancing or perhaps a game of *mora*; there was also a large table for playing *briscola* [two popular card games]. Sometimes we would have a famous accordionist who would really liven things up, and the dancing and singing would begin, of course also unlicensed. On one occasion the police came knocking at the door, demanding to know what was going on. My father told them it was a celebration for a christening!

"The wine we sold was home-made: it's a fact that the wine made in Clerkenwell was unbelievably good; I remember being the little boy who would suck at the tube to fill the bottles, and I would get drunk with those occasional mouthfuls! The grapes were delivered in great horse-drawn carts from Covent Garden and each family would buy a number of boxes. Every year the families made their wine, and I remember having to squeeze past the two barrels at the bottom of our stairs. You could always hear the wine fermenting in the barrels. Even as a child I liked the wine. I remember once when I was 10 going down into the cellar, picking up a bottle and drinking from it. I spilt some of it on my vest, and my vest turned blue. When my mother started wailing "My boy, 'e's poison 'imself!", Mrs Calliendo, an English lady who spoke Italian well, rushed over to help, saying "*Cos'è successo?*". It turned out that I had drunk methylated spirits; fortunately I had spilled more than I had swallowed!

"Our lodgers came from all over Italy, from the Romagna, Tuscany, Piacenza, Naples, etc. Some of them had travelled all over the world, constantly on the move looking for a place to settle. I used to sit and listen to them talking about Canada, Australia and many other countries. They would return to Italy every few years to see that their families were all right and take them money – some had no intention of ever returning permanently. I enjoyed listening to their conversation; these men had many different trades: some were waiters and there were also asphalters, plaster statuette makers and parquet floor layers.

Pino Maestri with Coach & Horses team and supporters

"On summer evenings we would sit outside the house and be entertained by travelling musicians. When relatives or friends of my mother came to London the talk would be of Lugagnano, my mother's village. My father came from Cremona and as I listened I could picture the streets and homes of the families in that small town.

"There were many Irish families living in the quarter: the Sullivans, the Connors, the Seymours and the Traceys, all an integral part of our Quarter, an area where, in our minds, we were embraced in a safe enclosure, our limits King's Cross Road, the Angel and Upper Street. Beyond these boundaries we had to look out for ourselves, but within the Quarter we had what I can best describe as the 'open door families' where everyone knew everyone and as children we could safely play out late in the streets.

"The young lads in the community almost without exception were mad about football. A game would start in Back Hill; we couldn't afford a proper ball so we would make one of rags or paper, scrunching up the materials until they were firm and resembled a ball. We would play for hours, running up and down the cobbled streets. And by the end of the game there would be 15 or 20 a side. Even later in life football was important.

In the summer months cricket would be played along Warner Street, where the road was flat, using a lamp-post as the wicket and a flat piece of wood for a bat and if we were lucky someone would produce a ball. There was usually an audience of bystanders. One particular man spent his days leaning against a bollard at the corner of Warner Street and Eyre Street Hill, where he would stand all day long, and, to while away the time roll a penny up and down the crease on the top of the bollard. Watching the antics of the cricketers must have lightened some of the monotony of his day!

"Half way down Little Saffron Hill opposite the school entrance was a sweet shop, Gasparo's (p 90), where we made stops on our way to school if we had any money, which wasn't too often.

"We would often go up to *Cura's*, the pet shop in Coldbath Square, where we would be amused by the lizards, frogs and snakes in their glass cases. Later we would perhaps go along Eyre Street Hill and harass Sam Perella, the ice-man who always sat outside his shop on the corner of Summers Street and who, if you upset him, would obligingly chase after you with his ice pick. I remember once,

Sam Perella and family outside their ice store in Summers Street

as we knocked on Perella's door, the old man came out and chased me up the street and, being such a clever boy, I turned my head to see if he was still coming and ran straight into a lamp post. I still have the scar on my forehead.

St Peter's Italian School

"The infant classes were mixed, but as we progressed to primary school the girls were taught in classrooms downstairs and the boys upstairs, though we continued to share the small rooftop playground. We were taught the basic curriculum and there was little chance of continuing school after the age of 14. If you were above average you could sit an exam at Hugh Myddelton School, a Central School nearby. I passed the exam but my parents wanted me to go to work. The only boys I remember who went on to Hugh Myddelton were Festa and Arturo Bonfanti.

The headmaster of St Peter's, Mr Taylor, was a football fanatic and his main ambition was for St Peter's to have a good football team, which he succeeded in doing. I remember that many times during the week he would come into Mr Delaney's class and say: "First team practice!" and Mr Delaney would go barmy because we were being taken from his class to play football. We would practise on the sloping asphalt rooftop playground.

"We were too good for the Holborn & District sports so we moved up to Islington & Borough where, to our amazement, we came second in our first year. I remember once we played against a team representing Middlesex Roman Catholic Boys' Relay Team at Motspur Park. There was myself, Dino Bacuzzi, Mario Salvoni, Nino Esposito and Arturo Bonfanti, and we represented the whole district. Mr Taylor was so keen we should excel at sport that he would take us into the school hall and run the boys around; the boy who came in last would get a whacking with the cane to liven us all up a bit.

"Mr Leaper took a class of boys newly arrived from Italy who spoke no English. We called it the Lunatic Class. Mr Leaper had to enlighten them concerning English ways and teach them the English language. They drove him mad.

"The school would send us for a fortnight's holiday in Hastings, where we would stay with 'aunties,' five or six children per lodging-house. This cost our families 12 shillings, a lot of money in those days, which they paid at the rate of sixpence a week. Italians who moved to the Barnsbury Estate, over Pentonville Road, and consequently mixed more with English people, went hop-picking in Kent in the summer where they would be paid according to how many baskets of hops they picked. I never went – to my mind it was a dismal affair, living in huts and washing in the open.

My youth

"After we left school our main pastime was dancing. Eight to twelve of us boys would dress up smartly and go out, three or four nights a week, to places like the Drill Hall, Judd Street, Kennington Halls and a little place called Itro's at Camden Town. Dances were even held round the back of Pentonville Prison, run by the warders. My best friends were Nino Esposito, Saba Bruschini, Titch

Corano, Guido Cotomini, Jimmy Falco and Aldo Salvoni (now my brother-in-law), who looked a bit like Clark Gable in those days. We were known as 'The Italian Boys', and romance was in the air. We were smartly dressed with trilby hats, big coats and jackets and perhaps a blue serge suit or a pinstripe, or a 'parson's grey' with 22-inch turned up bottoms, off we would go.

"When I was younger I sometimes went to Patsy Hearn's on a Sunday to hire a bicycle for tuppence a day and we rode up and down Hatton Garden. Occasionally some of us would hire bicycles for a whole day and ride to Hastings. Eli Sidoli was the best cyclist among us and always got there first.

"Later we started buying cars. We had only one driver – Jimmy Wise – but we each chipped in a few pounds and four of us bought first a Chrysler for £12. It was a beautiful car with a drop top. We then bought an old Clyno for £4. The mudguard was held on with an electric flex. Next was on old two-seater Buick for £8 and a Vauxhall 8-seater, like a limousine. Petrol was less than a shilling a gallon. Each year we would have a new car and we really used those cars.

Sat'dy morning pictures

"The Globe cinema at 12-15 Skinner Street, originally known as The People's Picture Palace was the favourite haunt of old and young alike. It was given many derogatory names, like 'the flea pit' or 'the bug'. The old Italians called it 'La Pipi'. There were 650 seats. The audience would show their reaction by cheering or booing. We would forever be bunking in, getting thrown out, then getting in again, leaving the latch up for the other boys to creep in. The cinema attendants had a hard time keeping the exuberance of the children at bay. Every half-hour they would discharge a large flit spray containing a sweet-smelling disinfectant into the heavy, fetid atmosphere.

"The doors were flung open at the end of the programme and the boys and girls would tear off down Skinner Street. All the boys would gallop at a hell of a pace, slapping their backsides, each one of them a budding Tom Mix. On weekday afternoons the Italian women could be seen making their way to the Pipi, to escape for a few hours from their drab everyday lives into Hollywood films of romance, passion and comedy, and coveting the glamour and luxury of the lifestyles portrayed on the screen. The Globe was the main source of entertainment for the Mammas and the Papas of the Italian Quarter at that time."

Film stars Ramon Navarro, Rudi Valli and the Barrymore family were the screen idols of the day and on the female side Greta Garbo, Ginger Rogers, Lucille Ball and Norma Shearer. The music of Jeanette Macdonald and Nelson Eddie, Bing Crosby with his *boodee-o-doos* brightened their days. In 1951 The Globe became The Rio. The doors closed on 29 October 1955, bringing to an end memories of Saturday morning matinees, price 1d, and the *Mammas'* dreams of looking like Hedy Lamarr or Lana Turner and being romanced by Robert Taylor or Clark Gable.

The Tortora family of Bakers Row: the asphalter's story

Remo Tortora started in the asphalt trade when he was 15 years old. He was following a long family tradition. He describes the trade as follows:

"It was very hard work and the Italians took great pride in their work. It was a skilful trade and the skills were handed down from generation to generation within families – the Lusardi, Franchi, Celeste, Enfissi, Boglione, Berni, and Reggio families, to name but a few. The best-known companies employing mostly Italians were Excel, Ragusa, Lawford and Natural Rock, Faldo's Rock Asphalt, and Val de Travers.

"If you were good at the trade, you could earn a good living, but the snag was the long spells away from home, which meant leaving your family. My father was sent to Leeds, Birmingham, Southampton, Liverpool and Wales, long distances in those times. The men were relatively happy on the job, their workmates were mostly friends from same environment and with that common factor, 'Down the 'Ill'.

"Mastic asphalt was mostly a natural material which came from Trinidad. It was shipped to England where it was heated, limestone and grit were added, and then it was formed into 56-pound blocks. It was then reheated to its melting point, about 230°C, usually directly on the building site, in large pots or mixers. The asphalt was laid with wooden floats by the skilled spreaders. Before 1956 coke and wood were used to make the fire under the pots. Not all the Italians became spreaders; some were trained to be mixers or potmen. The training usually took place on the building sites over about 6 months. In the early days when coke and wood were used they had to get up at about 4 am, as the asphalt had to be ready for 8. But with the introduction of bottled butane gas after the 1955 Smoke Abatement Act, they didn't have to get up quite so early. On each job there would be a charge-hand spreader, a second spreader, one potman or mixer, a labourer and an apprentice.

"The spreaders taught their skills to the young Italians and it took many years to learn the craftsmanship of a top man. The men were paid by the hour, depending on how much asphalt would be laid in a day. This was a compulsory amount, laid down by the companies with the agreement of the men, through the union.

"After WW II there was plenty of work available in the trade. Men who knew the game were happy to introduce their sons into the companies, as their fathers had done before them. On the whole they loved the work in the fresh air, the great sense of camaraderie and, at the end of the day, the satisfaction of a job well done.

The type of work available in the late 1940s was flat roofing, hospital floors, prisons, etc., tanking out building foundations, water tanks, car parks and roads.

"When the population of the Italian community decreased, so there were fewer Italian asphalters, and by the 1960s the trade had become less Italian dominated. Most Italians leaving school at this time had received a better education than their forebears and were seeking better jobs, cleaner and less physical work."

Tony Repetati, asphalt expert

Eugenio Repetati had married Anna Rossi in the village of Morfasso before they came to London in the late 1800s and lived at No.17 Back Hill. Eugenio found work in the asphalt trade. They had six children, the sons all following their father into the trade.

Antonio, born in 1894, served in the Italian army during WW I. He was taken prisoner by the Germans but 9 months later the camp he was in was overrun by the Allies and he returned home to his family in Back Hill. In 1921 he married Domenica Moglia, whose family came from Parma. She was a young waitress who lived just round the corner in No.4 Leicester Place. Their first home was No.4 Little Saffron Hill and the couple had three children, Antonio, Esther and Angela. Their only move was to council flats in Margery Street, off King's Cross Road, a nice block where they had a ground-floor flat. They were happy with the move as several Italian families who lived there had like themselves moved from the Italian Quarter, which was by now little more than an undesirable slum. At the time of writing (2010) the youngest daughter Angela, now aged 80, still lives there, but alone, as her siblings married long ago and left home.

A tribute to Tony from Whitbreads, the company where he worked for over 40 years:

One of the most familiar figures at Chiswell Street [Finsbury] for the past 40 years and more is Mr Antonio Repetati – but he has never been on the company payroll. For Tony has been with the contracting firm of Val de Travers since he left school aged 14 in 1910. And for most of that time he has been his firm's representative under contract to carry out maintenance work at the Brewery.

Recently, to mark his long service at the Brewery, Tony had the rare distinction, as a non-member of the Company, of being presented with a commemorative tankard by Assistant Brewery Manager, Mr David Jones.

Every morning he sets out from his home in Margery Street, King's Cross, for the Brewery where he makes sure that all the asphalting work is in first-class condition. Something of an expert on beer as well as wine, he is also an enthusiastic cook, particularly interested in nature foods. Now that he is approaching his 72nd birthday, he has to give up more strenuous pastimes like swimming, on which he used to be very keen.

Tony's one regret was that, apart from his war service in the Italian Army in 1914, he never returned to Italy and never visited his father's birthplace, Morfasso, in the mountains of Northern Italy.

Margaret Moloney, long-term teacher at St Peter's School, tells her story

"It was the summer of 1930 and I had just left College. Jobs were hard to get so I was very pleased to receive a letter offering me 2 weeks' supply teaching at the "Italian School, EC1". "Better find out where it is", said my father. So, we took the tram to King's Cross and clanked along Farringdon Road to Back Hill. After some difficulty we located "St Peter's Italian School" round the corner from the church. "Doesn't look much like a school," said my father, gazing dubiously at the grimy surroundings. Indeed it didn't, rising straight from the narrow, cobbled street and resembling, if anything, the dark and shuttered warehouses nearby. "I don't think it's really suitable", said my father, but I was anxious to start work. "It's only for a fortnight", I urged. So I came to Clerkenwell for 2 weeks and stayed for 40 years! And when I retired left part of my heart behind.

"Next morning I approached my first post with excitement and some apprehension. In the bright sunshine of an August morning Saffron Hill, as Herbal Hill was then called, looked more cheerful. The street was full of children milling about. A big boy stood at the top of a few steps ringing a large brass hand bell. "You a new girl?", he asked as I approached, "can't come in here. This is the teacher's door". "I am a teacher", I said with dignity. He let me pass somewhat doubtfully. I didn't blame him. I was small and looked very young, I expect.

"Sister Agnes from the Convent next to the Church met me at the top of the stone steps. Dressed in the blue habit of the Sisters of Charity with the white-winged starched headdress of the time, she greeted me kindly, handing me keys and register and showing me my classroom. Alas, the Convent has gone and a photographer's studio stands in its place. I can never pass it without remembering the wonderful hard-working nuns leading such Spartan lives as they served the Italian community in those far-off days.

"The school was a tall, narrow building with an extra wing built on, called for many years 'the new part'. On the top floors was the Boys' Department under Mr Taylor. They had the privilege of using the roof playground and we girls, in the middle, chanted our spelling and tables while the boys playing football thundered overhead. And wonderful teams they produced on their cramped and inadequate ground. Old boys have come from across the world enquiring for the team photos that used to hang in the corridors. Alas, they were lost, like so much else, in the last war.

"The girls and infants played in a tiny yard sandwiched between the school, the Church, the Convent and a factory. It was like being at the bottom of a well-shaft as we gazed upward at a patch of sky. A heavy iron fire escape ran up the middle to the roof playground and the small area remaining was still further reduced by the row of outdoor lavatories that stood against one wall. Impossible to keep clean, they froze in winter and smelt in the summer – despite all the school keeper's efforts, poor man!

"In winter he had twenty or so coal fires to clear out every evening, re-lay and light again each morning. Wood and coal (in buckets) had to be lugged up ninety steep stone stairs from basement to roof – and fires had to be refuelled at least twice a day.

"Most of the children lived within a stone's throw of the school – Corporation Buildings, Farringdon Road Buildings, the Bourne Estate, Victoria Dwellings – some of them now swept way in the name of slum clearance. Living conditions were harsh and there was considerable poverty, but these old buildings were actually models in their day, infinitely better than the hovels they replaced and some of which still existed in the Quarter. What wonderful families came out of those old Dwellings, giving tremendous loyalty to the Church and School.

"Below ground in the school was a large hall reserved for the Girls and Infants. There we drilled, danced, performed plays, held parties and every December arranged a great Christmas Bazaar. When the blitz struck London the hall was strengthened and used as a shelter for bombed-out people.

"But of course the highlights of the year were the children's First Communion Day and Procession Sunday. Everybody 'walked', from 4-year-olds to girls and boys of 14. As the great day drew near the school overflowed with white frocks, veils, cloaks of many hues, wreaths, emblems, banners and flowers. And to the sound of the bands, we made our way through the packed streets decorated with garlands and with small altars and shrines in many windows.

"The great moment came as the statue of Our Lady of Mount Carmel swayed down Back Hill and flocks of doves were released to wheel overhead. At the close, Benediction was given from the steps of the Church and then, exhausted but thankful that all had gone well, we teachers retired to enjoy a sumptuous tea in the Convent while the crowds danced and sang far into the evening in the streets outside."

When Margaret Moloney retired after 40 years at the school, the last 15 years as headmistress, she was presented with a gift and a Papal award by Father Michael Power, Rector of SS Peter and Paul Church in nearby Amwell Street.

Pope honours headmistress

Miss Margaret Moloney, headmistress of St. Catherine Labouré Roman Catholic Primary School, Herbal Hill, Clerkenwell, is presented with a gift and a Papal award to mark her retirement by Father Michael Power, Rector of SS Peter and Paul Church, Amwell Street. Miss Moloney served for 40 years at the school, the last 15 years as headmistress. A reception, attended by pupils, parents, teachers and parishioners, was held for Miss Moloney at Finsbury Town Hall. She was presented with the Papal award "Bene Merenti" and a cheque from parents, pupils and staff. 28-7-70

Papal award for teacher Margaret Moloney

The Rapaciolis

Alberto Rapacioli with his ice cart

Alberto Rapacioli came to England in the 1930s. His family rented rooms in Summers Street, where he lived with his father Giuseppe, a tailor, and his two brothers Pino and Dino. Unfortunately Giuseppe was a little too fond of the bottle, came home one night the worse for wear, fell down the stairs of the house in Summers Street, and died.

Alberto married his Cristina, who was from the small village of Rustigazzo, not far from Morfasso. They married in St Peter's Italian Church and had three sons: Pino, Mario and Dino. They were reasonably comfortable because Alberto, who was an iceman, worked for Carlo Gatti, a major player in the importation and distribution of ice.

Alberto would haul huge blocks of ice in a horse-drawn cart and deliver them all around London. Fortunately he was a strong man. He had to drag the huge blocks of ice, grabbing them with a large pincer-like tool, up to a sack on the tailboard of the lorry, then, bending down and dragging the sack off the cart onto his back, take it into the shop or restaurant to which it was destined.

Unexpectedly, as Alberto arrived at work one morning, the boss pressed a card into his hand. It was a driving licence. He had never had a driving lesson in his life but used the lorry from then on. This made the job a little easier, though he had grown fond of the horses and was sorry to see them go.

144

In 1939 word came from a relative who still lived in Italy to say that Cristina's mother was terminally ill. She and the children hurried back to her old home in Rustigazzo in order to look after her mother. To everyone's dismay the war in Europe broke out and she and her children were unable to return to England. Italy soon came into the war, making matters a lot worse for everyone concerned. Many London Italians were stranded in Europe.

As the war went on, Alberto was called up into the British army, but he refused to take up arms against the country where his family lived, and in which he was born. He was adamant: "I'm Italian and I won't fight against Italy." He was a conscientious objector. For a time he was imprisoned, and afterwards interned on the Isle of Man.

In his son Dino's words: "We remained in Italy and lived for a while in the village of Variano, where my father's family owned a house and property. One day my mother, who was known to speak a little English, was approached by the *Capo* (head of the partisans in the area), who said: "If you will take in three injured English officers, I will attempt to get you extra food so that you can feed them." But in no time the Germans arrived in the village. Cristina hustled the English officers up to the attic. Just as well, because she was soon made to take in three German officers. The airmen in the attic

Certificate of Commendation for Cristina Rapacioli signed by Alexander

had to live a very quiet life while young Dino, who was about 6 years old, would be given a bucket covered with a rag and told to go upstairs and clean the rails. Of course, the bucket contained food for The English officers. When the Germans retreated the partisans came and took the officers to a place of safety. If the Germans discovered the Englishmen, they would have killed all the officers as well as my mother. When the British Government learned of her bravery, she was presented with a certificate signed by Field-Marshal Alexander.

"My mother and we children returned to England in February 1946. I was 9 years old. The channel crossing was horrendous, it was stormy with black skies and lashing rain, everyone was sick, and it took six hours. We were so happy when we finally saw the white cliffs of Dover. The train bringing us to London was the Golden Arrow. When we were finally seated on the train, we were so excited at the thought of seeing my father again, we soon forgot the dreadful crossing we had experienced. On the final stage of our journey, as the train pulled into the station, we could already smell the dust and dirt of the metropolis and hear the noise and bustle of the station. As the train stopped, my mother and I were looking out of the window and my mother pointed to a vaguely familiar-looking man waiting on the platform and said "*Ecco papa!*", "Look! there's your father!" I still get very emotional when I think of the moment I first set eyes on my father after six long years.

"In our absence, my father had moved out of 'the Hill', from Summer Street to Highbury, and was renting much better accommodation. I was sent to St John's Primary School where I received a good education, passed the Eleven Plus and won a place at Finchley Grammar School. In the evenings I would sit with my father and brother and he would tell us stories of the Italian Quarter in the 1940s. Apparently there was a group of Black Shirts, radicals, men who held ideas

Racing men with the comedian Max Miller (in top hat) in the 1930s

different from the general run. During the war years Cockneys in the area always referred to Italians as 'raddies'. My father could well have been called a raddie, as he lived by his own laws. Anyone stepping out of line 'down the Hill', for instance taking liberties with elderly people, stealing other people's property or bullying in general, would be receive a visit from my father and his friends and be told to behave "or else!".

"After the war, there were hostile feelings towards the Italians 'down the Hill'. My father told me about the racing gangs who, he said, were no threat to the Italian community in general. They were Italian bookmakers who moved into horseracing all over the country, pushing other bookmakers out and taking over their pitches. This created a lot of violence in the racing world.

"I met and married Silvia Narcisi in the Italian Church in 1959. From that date we both became involved with all the events in St Peter's Church, the bazaar, the procession, etc. We have two married children, Frank and Linda."

Alberto Cavalli: imprisonment, internment, and the Mazzini-Garibaldi Club

I was born in London, on 1 January 1923. My parents were Italian immigrants. My mother, Argia Ricci, was born in October 1899 and lived on a farm in the village of Muchio delle Corti, in the region of Emilia Romagna. She was referred to as a *contadina* (a farm girl). She came to London in 1913 to work for friends of the family who came from the same village, and had a successful business here.

My father, Calisto Maria Cavalli, was also born in Muchio delle Corti, on 11 March 1893. The Cavallis were a large family, nine in all, and Calisto had a very hard life. He had only three years of schooling and was largely self-taught. There was no work at all in his home region. He travelled the long road down into Southern Italy, to Puglia, where he worked in the mines, but he was very young and the work wasn't suitable.

Calisto returned home to his village. He decided to try his luck in England, where his uncle had a public house in Clerkenwell. Knowing that there would be a familiar face at the end of his journey made him less afraid of the adventure on which he was about to embark.

Calisto never looked back. His first job as a washer-up in a café taught him where the money lay. He observed the workings of the café trade and before long he had saved enough, found himself a partner, Giuseppe Rossi, and learned enough basic English to enable them to open a working men's "caff" in Upper Thames Street in the City. The business did so well that in no time at all they bought a second café, this time in Blackfriars Road. After a time they agreed to split up; Giuseppe kept the café in Upper Thames Street and Calisto the one in Blackfriars Road.

My parents married on 27 May 1922 and the marriage met with their relatives' approval, as they were from the same *paese*. Shortly after I was born in 1923 a baby brother, Edmundo, arrived. He was a delicate child, always ailing. A third child died in infancy, not unusual at the time, nevertheless very hard on my parents.

My mother, whose health had never been good, was unwell, so my father sent the three of us to Italy, in the hope that sunshine, good food and assistance from relatives would pick us up. I stayed with my mother and brother in the family home in Muchio delle Corti. There was a school in the village where I got at least three days' schooling a week.

We returned to England in 1931 when I was 8, but my mother's health never really improved, whilst Edmundo went from bad to worse. I spent many hours playing with him. Although sickly he was very bright, and we played card games by the hour. My father was kindly, but strict, and I was not allowed to play in the street like other boys in the neighbourhood. Education was paramount to my father and he paid for Edmundo and me to attend the Salesian College in Battersea, where we did well. Later, when the (Fascist) Italian Government opened a fee-paying school, *Istituto del Littorio*, it paid off and by the time we left I was fluent in French and also in correct Italian. In the evenings I helped my father in the café.

Life was pretty good in the years that followed. My father worked hard,

Alberto Cavalli and others in the (Fascist) holiday camp in Cattolica

opening the café at 6 in the morning and rarely closing before 8 pm. He was keen for me to keep up with my Italian grammar. He particularly wanted me not to forget my Italian roots, so off I went to St George's Roman Catholic evening classes. In order to attend that school you had to be a 'Tesserato', i.e. a member of the Party. Then you could go to the *fascio*, not because you had any political notions, but because of the need to keep together with your own kind. At that time, foreigners were not looked on kindly in England. It was difficult to integrate, so naturally we kept to ourselves. I loved dancing, so I went dancing in the official *fascio* Italian clubs. The first one was in Greek Street, Soho. Later they bought a beautiful place in Charing Cross Road.

Young Italians from all over the world were sent to Italy for a holiday to grow strong in the sunshine. We set off to Cattolica, a seaside resort near Rimini, for the *colonia*, which was a kind of holiday camp, subsidised by the Italian government. The first two weeks were spent on a replica of a ship made in concrete, where we mixed with young Italians from all over the world. We all wore

148

a uniform, consisting of a black shirt, white trousers and a sailor-type hat. This was of course a Fascist outfit, but we simply looked on it as a rather military type of boy scout holiday. The various groups had leaders, big fellows, who stood no nonsense and were very strict. We used to take turns on guard duty; they supplied us with make-believe guns and we patrolled the perimeter of the camp. We rested in the afternoons when it was too hot for fun on the beach. After two weeks we went to Rome where we were taken to see the wonders of the capital. Everyone enjoyed these holidays in the sun, and it was all down to Mussolini.

Galissi (centre), a well-known accordionist from 'down the Hill' with a group of internees on the Isle of Man

WW II was a devastating time for our little family. We were all right for the first year, then came the unexpected, devastating news – Italy had entered the war on the side of Hitler.

Action against aliens was swift: the custodian of enemy property took over all the clubs. Churchill's oft-repeated order, "Collar the lot!", caused great trauma to our little family. Without any warning the police turned up at our café in Blackfriars Road and took my father away on 14 June 1940, and the next day they came for me. My poor mother and Edmundo, whose health was worsening day by day, were left to cope as best they could. But poor Edmundo died a short time later, leaving my mother entirely alone.

My father and I were in different camps and we did not meet again for two years. My first taste of internment was Brixton prison, where I remained for 6 months, aged 16, then off to the Isle of Man. Eventually my father was transferred here too. We were treated reasonably well and had quite a pleasant time, except of course for missing our families.

There were games of football and a choir, the men put on shows, and with so many chefs the food was pretty good. There were lots of friends, boys I had gone to school and grown up with. Though it was not a bad life for us youngsters, for men like my father who had left a wife and a sick child at home it was a very difficult time, and there were many family men like him, suffering the same anxieties.

Finally, the camp which had held 3,000 people dwindled as they started to release the men. It had at last been realised that there were very few true Fascists among us. Most were only working-class people – those who had got involved with the Fascists had done so only because if you wanted business done in Italy you had to go to the Consulate to get the necessary papers, and the first thing they would ask was "*Sei Tesserato?*". If you were not a member you would end up at the end of the queue.

When the war ended, the Mazzini-Garibaldi Club reopened. Previously it had been a sort of mutual assistance society where people paid in so much a week, and when you needed medical assistance they would reimburse you. It was originally opened in 1861 in Laystall Street, right near the church, but in 1933 the Italian Government lent money and it moved to Red Lion Street. I was the youngest and am the only surviving member of the 20 men who helped reopen the Club in 1946-7, when the confiscated premises were released. However, we couldn't continue as a mutual assistance society when the National Health Service was established, so the club reopened as a social centre. Its proper name was actually the *Societa' per il Progresso degli Operai Italiani in Londra* (Society for the Progress of Italian Workers in London).

My wife's uncle, Serafino Pini, was the main promoter of this action. He assembled a crowd of supporters who each put down £25, and I was voted in as treasurer. All Italians wanted to join and the money rolled in. Membership cost £1 a week. There was dancing on Thursday, Saturday and Sunday, and many couples met there for the first time. It was here that I met my wife, Olga Besagni. The club was always so packed that you could hardly move, but gradually it lost its attraction for the youngsters, who had other distractions: television, cars, etc. The start of another era.

Collini family

Augusto Collini with van in 1929

Giovanni Collini was the first Collini to settle in the Clerkenwell area. In 1900, he arrived in London from Pinzolo, a small town in the Rendena Valley of Northern Italy, at that time under Austrian rule. He was a craftsman, specialising in grinding knives. He spoke no English, but he quickly established himself with the butchers around Smithfield Market and was able to build up a business..

In 1914, Giovanni brought his 13-year-old son Augusto to London; he immediately began working as a knife-grinder with his father, learning the craft as he went along. Together, they wheeled their grinding-barrow around the City of London and, by 1929, Augusto was able to buy his own van in order to cover a wider area.

In 1930, Augusto returned to Pinzolo, where he met Maria, also a Collini – it was a common surname in the area – and they got married three months later. Returning to London, they lived in King's Cross Road, where their first son Armo was born in 1931.

In 1932 they purchased a house named Grosvenor House at 109 Guilford Street from another Collini, Daniele, and went into the bed & breakfast business.

Maria worked tirelessly to run Grosvenor House, while Augusto continued to expand his knife-grinding business. During World War II, Grosvenor House was home to scores of G.I.s and Canadian Servicemen. Augusto's van was requisitioned and he had to return to pushing a grinding barrow around the streets. However, he was lucky not to be interned like most Italians in the area.

After the War, Augusto passed on his skills to his sons Armo and Alfonso, and the three of them continued to work together for many years. In the early 1970s, Alfonso moved to Italy.

Maria Collini outside Grosvenor House, 1930s

In 1986, a long tradition at Grosvenor House came to an end when Augusto and Maria retired and moved to Mill Hill. The knife-grinding business was continued by Augusto's son, Armo, and continues today through Armo's son, Robert. That's four generations of Collini grinders, still serving the City of London.

The Collini family has always maintained very strong ties with St Peter's Italian Church, Clerkenwell Road. The Collinis have been involved, in one way or another, in all the Church's activities and social events, from being founder members of the OGI (the Olympics for Young Italians) through to providing polenta and sausages at the annual Sagra (the Clerkenwell Italian Festival).

Among Giovanni Collini's descendants are very many professional sons and daughters, skilled and determined workers, musicians and artists, all with the same spirit of adventure and gusto for life.

From its humble origins in a beautiful but poor valley in Italy, the Collini family has spread out to different parts of the globe; but Little Italy and the Italian Community in London remain at the centre of it.

Giovanni Luigi Ferrari, 'Il Maestro', 1849-1933

When Giovanni Ferrari arrived with his parents in 1880 at his destination, Clerkenwell, he was welcomed by both school and church. He was a fit young man and very clever, which would be of huge benefit to the inhabitants of the colony, young and old alike. Many Italian immigrants were illiterate, and the outlook for them must have been pretty grim for those hoping to go into business or to work for English firms. Families were continually settling here and it was imperative that the children learn not only English but also correct Italian speech and grammar.

Few families spoke proper Italian, they used the dialect of their native province, which restricted them to a small number of social groups. Ferrari loved his work at the school and, as he walked through the quarter, he was recognised and acknowledged by everyone: "Good Morning, Maestro" could be heard continually, or alternatively: "*Buon Giorno, Maestro Ferrari*". He was happy and popular. He was earning a good salary, and paid the rates for two houses in Warner Street. He was constantly invited to events at the Consulate and the Embassy. He was also Secretary to the Italian Hospital in Queen Square. In 1884, at the age of 34, he married one of his pupils, Angela Zermani, aged 17. They had five children: Giuseppe, Umberto, Marguerita (Daisy), Violet (Dolly) and Vittorio. Sadly, they lost Daisy, a beautiful girl, at the age of 27. She died of tuberculosis which was rampant and incurable at that time.

The Maestro died in 1933 and, as you can see from the obituary below, his funeral was a very big affair, with a Requiem Mass at the Italian Church. The cortège processed around the streets of the Quarter with a large following of Italians. He was buried at Finchley Cemetery.

Translation of the obituary

A Doyen of the Italians in London
At the age of 84, amidst great mourning by countless Italians who had known and loved him, Maestro Ferrari, who taught for over 50 years at St Peter's Italian School, passed away. Maestro Ferrari was a notable figure in our colony and was considered a doyen of London Italians, who embraced him with respectful and loving affection.

He was born in Borgotaro in 1849 and dedicated himself at a very early age to teaching. After only five years he was rewarded with a transfer to London, where he arrived in 1880. From that day onwards he never left the Italian schools in Little Saffron Hill, of which he eventually became Director. In 1900 he was honoured with the Silver Medal, L'Argento di Benemerenza and in 1925, in recognition of his 50 years of teaching, he was awarded the Gold Medal, which was conferred on him by the then Italian Ambassador, Marchese della Torretta.

On the day of his funeral a large crowd convened at St Peter's Church to pay their respects. Also present were representatives of the colony's Associations, together with their banners. The Secretary of the Fascio was represented by Camerata Perosino, along with a handful of Blackshirts with their pennants. There were many relatives and friends and a large group of pupils from the schools accompanied by the headmistress, Miss Baisi, and a teacher, Miss Pizzanelli. Among the school representatives was Signorina Tersilla Balestreri, who had collaborated with Maestro Ferrari over many years.

Olive Angiolina Besagni, née Ferrari, told by herself

My father, Giuseppe Ferrari, always known as Joe Ferrari, was the older of Maestro Ferrari's two sons. He went as a matter of course first to St Peter's Italian school and then aged 11 to the Salesian College at Battersea (see also pp 105, 148). Joe was mad about opera and football, but forgot all else when he met my mother Jeanetta Oxley at a social evening, held on Saturdays in rooms above St Peter's Italian church.

Netta Oxley, born in 1887 at 110 Goswell Road, was English, the youngest daughter of the Oxley family, who ran a chain of ironmongers shops across the country. At first she helped her mother in the shop on the corner of Goswell Road and Bastwick Street, but then became interested in her sister Helenora's dressmaking business, proving to be a gifted seamstress. When she saw young Joe Ferrari at the Church Social imitating Mr Pastry dancing The Lancers she laughed so much and was so taken with him, there was nothing for it but to marry, against much opposition on both sides. Such mixed marriages between Italian immigrant families and established English ones were not looked on with favour.

The couple married in 1910. They lived at first in Rosebery Avenue but in the 1920s moved to Elaine Grove in Gospel Oak. I was born there in 1925, the youngest of five children. I was a happy, lively girl who ran, skipped, skated, did cartwheels, anything but walk; and I was overjoyed when my parents found the money for tap-dancing, ballet and piano lessons, though they were far from rich. My pocket money was a halfpenny a week, we lived in a 3-room flat on the upper floor of a two-storey house, and shared toilet facilities in the garden with the family living below on the ground floor. But Netta's clever needle kept me well dressed.

In 1936 the family moved to Constantine Road in Hampstead. I did well in the 11-plus exams and passed into the educationally progressive Fleet Road School, which I loved. When war broke out in 1939 the school was evacuated to Exton in the county of Rutland, where I had a great time acting, singing, dancing and writing sketches for performance in the village hall. As no bombs dropped in London after a year, my parents brought me home, to a life centred on the Parliament Hill Lido – as the weather was perfect! There was no more schooling, and my parents tried to get me to apply for an office job. Then, almost by chance I came into contact with Italians for the first time because an old friend of my father's offered me a job painting eyes, lips and gold trim on religious statuettes being made at Pagliai's factory in Great Sutton Street, off Goswell Road.

Most of the workers there were Italian. The older men had been taught by my grandfather, Maestro Ferrari, at evening classes and they remembered him with affection. Amongst the younger men was a 16-year-old boy called Bruno Besagni, who worked as an artistic sprayer.

At 18, I became a trainee negative cutter at the Realist Film Unit, a small documentary company in Dean Street, then moved on to Pathé in Wardour Street as Assistant Editor to Alexander Milner Gardner, amongst other tasks rescuing newsreels stored at Elstree long before the war. I loved that job, it was creative. We

Bruno Besagni putting the finishing touches to his reproduction of the Madonna and Child that is carried in the annual Procession

also worked as one of the teams covering the wedding of Princess Elizabeth and Philip Mountbatten. We worked all night – it was a race to be the first company to get out a complete film of it. We won! But then I married Bruno in July 1948 (to the great joy of my father), and in the course of time became pregnant with Anita and had to leave the job. Two years later our son Tony was born. When Anita was five years old Mr Gardner invited me back to Pathé. My mother-in-law Anita looked after the children and I went back to work full-time, with Bruno's blessing. Bruno had all this time remained in the statuette-making business.

All went well, but then my boss Alex was taken ill and died. I stayed on at Pathé for a while, but the time had come for my mother-in-law Anita to go to America and visit her daughters (p 125), so it was back to being a housewife for me.

Coda

After Maestro Ferrari died the Ferrari family dispersed in various directions. Angela was happy to continue living with her daughter's family when her husband the Maestro died. Until then the Maestro had remained in touch with the Italian School, the Italian Hospital and St Peter's Italian Church, but afterwards the family had little to do with the activities 'down the Hill'. Daughter Dolly, husband Harry and their four children Gordon, Stella, Gloria and Victor lived in the upper storeys of a house in River Street. I called on them quite often on my way home from work in the 1950s.

The demise of the *Quartiere* was slow despite the destruction of its old buildings, because the Italians keep returning to the Church, the Procession, and the Italian shops. Many have wonderful memories of it, despite the memories of poverty and horrors like fighting the filth, the lice, the bugs and the vermin, without the aid of the detergents and cleaning agents that are so easy to come by today. Their mainstay was huge bars of Sunlight Soap, carbolic and washing soda, that left the hands red and sore. As WW II drew to a close, the slum clearance programme that had begun in the 1930s accelerated. The houses that had sheltered laughter and drama were now empty shells, except for a small cluster of prefabs between Bath Street and Warner Street. Black holes replaced what had once been windows with cheeky little dark, curly-headed children peering out to watch their big brothers play interminable games of football – for there were few cars driving through the Hill in the old days to disrupt the game, only the regular clip-clop of horses and carts making their collections and deliveries.

Some of the old life remains, though mostly in people's memories. The prefabs have gone and the old buildings have been replaced by luxury apartments and penthouses. These are mostly occupied by affluent young city workers who live there only on weekdays, and at weekends retire to their homes in the country. But all comes to life once in the year: at the time of the great Procession in the middle of July, richly illustrated by anecdote and photographs in the course of this book.

Index

* = illustration
PH = public house